Alpine Linux Administration

Definitive Reference for Developers and Engineers

Richard Johnson

Contents

5

Introduction

Alpine Linux has emerged as a distinctive and influential distribution within the open-source ecosystem, primarily recognized for its emphasis on security, simplicity, and resource efficiency. Designed from the ground up with a minimalist philosophy, Alpine provides a robust platform tailored for modern computing environments ranging from embedded systems and virtual machines to large-scale cloud deployments and containerized microservices. This book offers a comprehensive guide to Alpine Linux administration, aiming to equip readers with the knowledge and skills necessary to expertly deploy, configure, and manage Alpine-based systems in diverse operational contexts.

The foundation of Alpine Linux is built upon carefully chosen components such as musl libc and BusyBox, which collectively contribute to its remarkably small footprint and high performance. Understanding these architectural choices is crucial for appreciating Alpine's behavior, compatibility considerations, and performance characteristics. Furthermore, a clear comprehension of Alpine's branching model, including the stable and edge release channels, provides administrators with insight into lifecycle management and update strategies suited for their specific use cases.

Installation and deployment form the cornerstone of any system administration task. This volume delves into an array of installation techniques ranging from traditional media-based methods to network-boot and cloud-integrated workflows. Additionally, it examines diskless and persistent storage modes, custom partitioning schemas, and automated headless installation approaches, thereby enabling efficient and reproducible system rollouts across physical and virtual infrastructures. Secure boot mechanisms and firmware considerations are also addressed to ensure compatibility and integrity in heterogeneous hardware environments.

Package management on Alpine Linux, centered on the apk toolchain, offers advanced capabilities for dependency resolution, repository management, and system customization. Mastery of these features is essential for maintaining system stability and security. The text explores strategies for package pinning, masking, and custom package construction with cryptographic signing, emphasizing practices that support reliability and compliance in complex deployments. Further, system state management, transactional updates, and rollback procedures are discussed to empower administrators with mechanisms that minimize downtime and operational risk.

Robust system configuration and service management underlie Alpine's operational integrity. This work investigates OpenRC init system in depth, alongside configuration file policies, user and privilege management, locale and time synchronization, and the orchestration of monitoring and logging frameworks. Complemented by essential backup strategies and system snapshot techniques, these topics collectively contribute to the creation of resilient environments.

Networking constitutes a critical domain where Alpine's flexibility and security converge. Comprehensive coverage includes interface configuration, advanced routing, VLANs, firewall implementation with nftables and iptables, VPN deployments, and intrusion detection tools. Guidance on securing network services such as SSH, DNS, and web proxies supplements this foundation, ensuring that systems remain protected against evolving threats.

Alpine Linux's suitability for containerization and orchestration is thoroughly examined with detailed insights into image optimization, container runtimes, Kubernetes integration, and container security layers. Automated workflows for building and publishing container images are presented with an emphasis on reproducibility and security compliance.

The pursuit of heightened security within Alpine environments extends through kernel hardening, Mandatory Access Control implementations, filesystem encryption, resource sandboxing, vulnerability scanning, and incident response strategies. These advanced topics equip administrators to safeguard systems against a broad spectrum of risks, applying contemporary best practices aligned with industry standards.

Finally, the book addresses diagnostic and recovery procedures essential for operational continuity. Techniques for troubleshooting boot issues, performance profiling, package resolution, network diagnostics, filesystem recovery, and forensics are presented. This reinforces the administrator's capability to maintain system health and respond effectively to incidents.

The closing chapters emphasize automation, scalability, and governance. They introduce configuration management frameworks, disaster recovery automation, policy enforcement, CI/CD integration, and forward-looking security paradigms including Zero Trust. These subjects reflect the evolving requirements of Alpine Linux deployments in enterprise and cloud-scale infrastructures.

This text is intended as a definitive resource for system administrators, security professionals, and DevOps engineers seeking deep expertise in Alpine Linux. By systematically presenting foundational concepts alongside advanced configuration and security techniques, the book aims to foster proficiency and confidence in managing Alpine Linux within diverse and demanding environments.

Chapter 1

Foundations of Alpine Linux

Alpine Linux is not just another distribution—it's a thoughtfully engineered platform designed to meet the distinct needs of today's lightweight, secure, and highly modular computing environments. This chapter unveils the building blocks that differentiate Alpine Linux from its peers, exploring its design ethos, technical underpinnings, and the vibrant community that propels its rapid evolution. Whether you're deploying containers at scale or securing critical infrastructure, understanding these foundations is your gateway to leveraging Alpine's full potential.

1.1. Alpine Linux Philosophy and Design

Alpine Linux embodies a distinct philosophy centered on three interwoven principles: security, simplicity, and resource efficiency. These pillars not only define its technical architecture but also guide community engagement, package management, and system customization, establishing a unique identity within the landscape of Linux distributions.

At the core of Alpine Linux's philosophy is an uncompromising commitment to security. Unlike conventional systems that retrofit security mechanisms onto general-purpose configurations, Alpine integrates security at every layer of the build process and runtime environment. The foundational choice to use musl—a lightweight, standards-compliant libc implementation—over the more ubiquitous glibc stems from a deliberate decision to reduce the attack surface and dependency complexity. musl's smaller codebase inherently presents fewer vulnerabilities and supports modern security features such as stack smashing protection out of the box.

Furthermore, Alpine Linux employs position-independent executables (PIE) and stack-smashing protection (SSP) consistently throughout its packages, enforcing compile-time hardening that mitigates buffer overflow exploits and return-oriented programming attacks. The kernel parameters and security policies are prudently configured by default, avoiding unnecessary services and disabling legacy protocols vulnerable to compromise. Such rigor extends into runtime components: the use of PaX and grsecurity patches (historically) and consistently minimal privileges adhere to the principle of least privilege, significantly reducing the risk surface exposed to potential attackers.

Simplicity constitutes the second foundational element, reflecting a minimalist design that eschews superfluous features and complexity. Alpine Linux adheres to the UNIX philosophy of "doing one thing and doing it well," visible in every strategic decision. This simplicity manifests in the base system, which includes only the necessities required to boot and operate, thereby minimizing dependencies and potential configuration conflicts. The default init system, OpenRC, follows a straightforward and transparent process supervision model, eschewing the complexity and monolithic nature of alternatives such as systemd.

The package management system apk is another exemplar of simplicity. Designed for rapid execution with minimal resource consumption, apk maintains a compact, indexed package database that supports both binary and source packages without excessive metadata or layering. The simplicity of apk enhances maintainability and reduces cognitive load when managing system components, enabling users and developers alike to understand and control the environment with precision.

Resource efficiency, the third guiding principle, is intricately connected to both security and simplicity. Alpine Linux targets environments where hardware constraints and performance are critical considerations, such as embedded systems, containerization platforms, and virtualized workloads. Achieving efficiency begins with the choice of tools and libraries optimized for minimal resource footprints. By leveraging musl and busybox—an amalgamation of Unix utilities in a single, compact executable—Alpine minimizes disk space usage and runtime memory demands.

This economy of resources also extends to runtime behavior. Alpine avoids running unnecessary daemons by default, reducing CPU overhead and improving system responsiveness. Its streamlined system services consume less memory and allow for faster boot times, critical qualities in dynamic cloud-native infrastructures and devices with limited computing capacity.

The interplay of these principles sets an architectural context for Alpine Linux that influences every technical and community decision within the project. Security mandates rigorous code audits and upstream package selection favoring stability and minimal attack vectors. Simplicity shapes repository curation and documentation practices, encouraging clarity and minimalism over excessive abstraction. Efficiency drives continuous profiling and optimization tasks, ensuring the distribution remains lean without sacrificing functionality.

Community governance reflects these values through a transparent development process that emphasizes peer review, reproducible builds, and minimalistic but comprehensive documentation. Contributors are encouraged to adhere to strict quality criteria that preserve Alpine's core principles, fostering a cohesive ecosystem aligned with the distribution's mission. This alignment guarantees that enhancements or new package inclusions serve the fundamental goals rather than bloat or introduce fragile complexity.

This philosophy has direct implications for Alpine Linux's adoption in security-critical applications and resource-constrained contexts. Its role in containerization platforms such as Docker is emblematic: the distribution's minimal size and hardened configuration reduce container image bloat and potential compromise vectors. The emphasis on simplicity enables rapid iteration and deployment without the overhead of cumbersome configuration or dependency resolution, fulfilling modern DevOps requirements for lightweight, secure, and efficient base images.

Alpine Linux's guiding principles act as a rigorous frame-work ensuring that security, simplicity, and resource efficiency are not merely aspirational goals but operational realities. These priorities justify architectural choices—from libc implementation, package compilation flags, and init system selection to community governance models—setting a firm foundation for all subsequent exploration of Alpine's technical attributes and ecosystem. Understanding this philosophical nexus is essential for appreciating how Alpine continuously balances innovation with minimalism to meet the stringent demands of contemporary computing environments.

1.2. musl libc and BusyBox Integration

The choice of core system components fundamentally shapes the performance, footprint, and flexibility of modern Linux-based environments, particularly within constrained or containerized settings. Opting for musl libc as the default C standard library alongside BusyBox for core userland utilities creates a synergy that addresses challenges of efficiency, size, and compatibility while preserving operational integrity.

musl libc: Design Principles and Impact

musl libc is an implementation of the C standard library tailored for static linking, thread safety, and minimal runtime overhead. Unlike the GNU C Library (glibc), musl maintains a clean, simple codebase with a focus on correctness and standards compliance. Key advantages include a smaller code footprint—musl is typically on the order of 400–600 KB, whereas glibc often exceeds multiple megabytes—and superior performance in static linking scenarios through reduced relocation complexity.

9

The impact of this on system performance manifests in faster program startup times and lower memory consumption. Static linking with musl eliminates external dependencies, enabling container images to remain lightweight and portable. This is particularly critical in cloud-native environments where rapid scaling and minimal attack surface are priorities. The lean design of musl also results in lower instruction cache pressure, which is beneficial in environments with limited CPU resources or embedded hardware.

Compatibility with legacy applications presents some challenges, as musl omits some glibc-specific extensions and less standardized behaviors. However, for most server and container workloads, strict adherence to POSIX and standard C interfaces ensures broad compatibility. Furthermore, musl often exposes more deterministic and sane behavior; for instance, its thread cancellation and locale implementations conform better to standards, resulting in more predictable and robust applications.

BusyBox: A Swiss Army Knife for Userland Utilities

BusyBox consolidates numerous Unix utilities into a single executable, dynamically dispatching to the appropriate functionality at runtime. This consolidation drastically reduces the binary size footprint compared to installing individual GNU Core Utilities, making it highly suited for minimal base systems and container images. A typical BusyBox binary ranges around 1 MB, whereas a full suite of equivalent coreutils binaries may exceed 10 MB combined.

This efficiency translates directly to faster container startup times and reduced disk I/O during image loading. For embedded server systems or lightweight containers, the ability to provide essential shell utilities (such as ls, cp, vi, and networking commands) without unnecessary complexity or bloat is crucial. BusyBox also supports static linking against musl libc, reinforcing the minimal dependencies paradigm.

Operational efficiency is enhanced as BusyBox's utilities are generally simpler and faster to execute, removing overhead caused by features rarely needed in basic administrative or initialization scripts. While not all advanced options available in their GNU counterparts exist, these compromises are deliberate and balanced against the benefits of reduced resource usage and greater predictability.

Integrative Benefits in Server and Container Use Cases

In server environments where resource efficiency and stability are paramount, integrating musl libc with BusyBox significantly reduces the base system footprint. For example, consider a minimal web server container running nginx statically linked with musl. The absence of glibc eliminates common sources of binary incompatibilities across distributions, simplifying deployment pipelines and reducing the risk of dependency conflicts.

Moreover, the combination reduces the attack surface—fewer libraries and simpler utility implementations mitigate vulnerabilities. The combined binary sizes result in container images that are substantially smaller (in many cases less than 30 MB), facilitating rapid provisioning and scaling on orchestrated clusters such as Kubernetes.

In embedded servers used in edge computing, the low memory usage and reduced CPU overhead of musl combined with BusyBox's minimal utilities allow systems to operate within strict hardware limits while maintaining robustness. Boot times improve, and runtime diagnostics remain available without relying on bulky toolsets.

Concrete Examples

A representative example includes building a container image for a microservice with the following components:

```
FROM alpine:latest

RUN apk add --no-cache busybox musl

COPY myservice /usr/local/bin/myservice

CMD ["/usr/local/bin/myservice"]
```

Here, BusyBox provides the core shell and utilities compatible with musl-based binaries such as myservice. The total image size remains under 10 MB, versus more than twice as large if using a glibc-based distribution with GNU core utilities.

Another scenario involves static linking:

```
musl-gcc -static -o myapp myapp.c
strip myapp
```

Linking the application statically against musl, combined with BusyBox's simplified utilities, yields an efficient deployment artifact, eliminating the need for external shared libraries and maintaining a reduced runtime environment.

Trade-offs and Future Directions

While the integration of musl libc and BusyBox aligns well with minimalism and efficiency goals, it is important to recognize limitations. Some complex applications requiring GNU-specific extensions or advanced locale support may exhibit incompatibilities or need patching. The relatively reduced feature set in BusyBox utilities may require supplementing in sophisticated environments.

Nevertheless, ongoing development in both projects addresses these gaps. Incremental extensions in `musl` improve compatibility with mainstream software, while `BusyBox` continues expanding its utility coverage. Hybrid approaches employing `musl/BusyBox` as the base and selectively layering standard GNU utilities as needed strike a practical balance.

The strategic adoption of `musl libc` with `BusyBox` exemplifies a pragmatic shift towards streamlined, efficient, and predictable foundational components. This combination fosters container and server environments optimized for rapid deployment, low resource utilization, and consistent behavior, coherent with modern infrastructure imperatives.

1.3. Architectural Overview

Alpine Linux distinguishes itself through a deliberately minimalist and modular core architecture, designed to support an extensible and composable operating system framework. The core architecture is centered on a small, efficient kernel, a compact userspace, and a set of modular system layers that enable aggressively minimal base systems while facilitating extensive customization. This architecture is optimized for diverse environments, ranging from embedded systems to large-scale container deployments, where resource constraints and security considerations heavily influence system design.

At the foundation lies the Linux kernel, statically configured and often patched for size, security, and performance. Alpine employs a monolithic kernel with selective modular loading capability; however, its usage patterns favor a kernel stripped of unnecessary drivers and features. This

offers a reduced attack surface and faster boot times, aligning with Alpine's overarching philosophy of simplicity and
security. The kernel is coupled with the musl C library
as the standard C library implementation. musl replaces
the more common GNU *glibc*, providing a lightweight,
standards-compliant implementation of the C library that
consumes fewer resources and improves static linking support. This substitution is pivotal in maintaining a minimal runtime footprint while preserving compatibility with
most software.

The system's userspace is centered around BusyBox, a single binary providing a multitude of standard Unix utilities. Unlike distributions that rely on separate binaries
for each command, BusyBox consolidates essential tools-
such as shells, file utilities, and network utilities-into one
compact package, significantly reducing disk and memory usage. Alpine's default shell is ash, provided by Busy-
Box, reinforcing the low-overhead design. This minimal
userspace is essential for Alpine's use in container environments, where image size directly translates to shipping
and deployment efficiency.

Logical separation and modularity extend beyond the kernel and userspace utilities into Alpine's package management and service layers. The apk package manager embodies the core modularity concept by enabling fine-grained
control over system components. It supports the installation of no more than the required packages-often a base
system as minimal as 2–3 MB-without sacrificing dependency resolution and system integrity. Packages in Alpine
follow a strict, minimal dependency policy: they are designed as small, focused units of functionality rather than
large monolithic collections. This modular packaging approach simplifies the assembly of custom system images
tailored precisely to the application requirements.

System components and services operate within an init system designed to be likewise minimal and modular: OpenRC. Unlike heavy, monolithic init systems, OpenRC focuses on simplicity, speed, and portability. It orchestrates service dependencies and parallelizes startup without introducing complex runtime overhead. This contributes toward rapid boot times and a small persistent memory footprint, critical in both embedded use cases and containerized environments.

Alpine's architectural philosophy incorporates the principle of composability through its layered design. The base OS layer provides the minimal runtime environment, while additional functionalities-such as networking stacks, language runtimes, cryptographic toolkits, and application frameworks-are introduced via discrete, purpose-built packages. This stratified layering allows administrators and build systems to compose custom Alpine-based environments. For instance, a container image can be constructed that includes only the Alpine base plus a specific curated runtime environment, significantly reducing attack surface, startup latency, and disk space usage.

An important aspect of Alpine's architecture is the adoption of the hardened toolchain and security features. The build system enforces Position Independent Executable (PIE) binaries and stack-smashing protection, yielding binaries with increased resistance to common exploitation techniques. As these features are integrated into every component, from shell utilities to kernel modules, the modular layers collectively benefit from system-wide security hardening, despite the base system's minimalism.

Moreover, Alpine supports diverse hardware architectures with consistent modularity and composability.

The repository structure and package metadata are architecture-aware yet unified, enabling straightforward cross-compilation and deployment. This enables Alpine to target systems ranging from 32-bit embedded processors to 64-bit cloud infrastructures without sacrificing its core architectural principles.

Alpine's core architecture is a cohesive integration of a minimal Linux kernel, a lightweight standard library, consolidated userspace utilities, a modular package management system, and a straightforward init framework. These components compose a highly configurable stack, enabling construction of minimal but resilient installations tailored to particular use cases. This modular and composable approach not only reduces resource consumption but also enhances security posture, deployment flexibility, and maintainability across diverse operating environments.

1.4. Alpine Edge vs Stable: Branching Model

Alpine Linux's branching model is fundamentally structured around two primary release channels: *Edge* and *Stable*. This dichotomy is central to how Alpine manages its software lifecycle, update mechanics, and risk profiles, providing system administrators with distinct strategic options suited for varied production environments and deployment strategies.

The Edge branch serves as Alpine's cutting-edge, *rolling-release* channel. It incorporates the latest package versions immediately after they pass the initial stages of community testing and integration into the development repository. Edge is in continuous flux-packages and kernel versions are updated frequently, sometimes daily, reflecting upstream developments almost in real time.

This continuous integration model ensures access to new features, security patches, and performance improvements as soon as they become available. Edge acts essentially as the *current development snapshot* of Alpine, rendering it ideal for users who prioritize having the newest software capabilities and are willing to engage actively with the system's maintenance.

However, this progression speed inherently introduces a higher risk profile. The lack of prolonged, extensive testing means that newly introduced packages or updates may harbor bugs, regressions, or compatibility issues not yet identified or resolved. Furthermore, the rapid change cadence demands frequent administrative oversight to manage dependency conflicts and package migrations.

Consequently, Alpine Edge is most appropriate for:

- Developers and testers requiring immediate access to the latest Alpine features.

- Use cases focused on preventing software stagnation where cutting-edge tools are critical.

- Experimental environments or continuous integration pipelines where system breakage carries minimal operational risk.

```
sudo apk update
sudo apk upgrade --available
```

```
fetch http://dl-cdn.alpinelinux.org/alpine/edge/main/x86_64/APKINDEX.tar.gz
(1/45) Upgrading busybox (1.34.1-r0 -> 1.36.1-r0)
(2/45) Upgrading musl (1.2.2-r0 -> 1.2.3-r0)
...
(45/45) Upgrading alpine-base (3.17.0-r0 -> 3.18.0-r0)
OK: 53 MiB in 120 packages
```

Contrastingly, the Stable branch adopts a *fixed-release* model. Alpine developers freeze package versions and assemble a well-tested release snapshot, which remains unchanged over a defined lifecycle. Updates within Stable are typically limited to security patches and critical bug fixes, eschewing feature updates or version upgrades that might cause incompatibilities.

Stable releases occur at scheduled intervals, approximately once every six months, and each release is supported with security and bug-fix updates for about three years. The measured and controlled approach ensures high software reliability and system stability, making Stable the branch of choice for production systems where availability and predictability are paramount.

Stable releases undergo rigorous quality assurance, including extensive testing against regression and compatibility. This systematic approach minimizes the risk of system disruptions caused by software updates, thereby lowering the administrative overhead and reducing unplanned downtime.

Typical deployment environments leveraging Stable include:

- Production servers and embedded devices requiring long-term stability.

- Environments with strict compliance and uptime requirements.

- Systems with limited maintenance resource availability.

Administrative updates in Stable focus predominantly on apk actions confined to security patches:

```
sudo apk update
sudo apk upgrade --available --security
```

This conservative update strategy aligns with minimizing change-induced risks while still maintaining a secure operational baseline.

The divergence in Alpine's branching model manifests clearly through their respective lifecycles:

- **Edge**: Unstable lifecycle, continuous inflow of updates, no predefined end-of-life. Administrators face ongoing challenges of ensuring system integrity amid an evolving codebase.

- **Stable**: Stable lifecycle, set release timetable, and lifecycle policy with defined support periods facilitating planning for upgrades and migrations.

Edge's rapid update cadence demands robust automation and monitoring frameworks to promptly detect and resolve faults. Conversely, Stable emphasizes a "set-and-maintain" philosophy where change management prioritizes preemptive validation.

The risk profile in Edge is higher, primarily stemming from exposure to possibly unvetted software changes, making it susceptible to regressions and dependency inconsistencies. Stable mitigates these risks via controlled updates but sacrifices immediate access to new features.

Informed decision-making regarding Alpine's branch usage depends on deployment requirements, operational constraints, and tolerance for system disruption:

- **Stability and Predictability**: Stable is unequivocally superior where uptime and predictable oper-

19

ation outweigh the need for the latest software versions.

- **Security Updates**: Both branches receive security patches; however, Stable filters updates more strictly, whereas Edge incorporates a broader scope of updates, which, while including fixes, may also transit unstable code.

- **Upgrade Frequency**: Edge demands more frequent system upgrades-a commitment to agile maintenance-while Stable enables longer periods between major version upgrades.

- **Compatibility and Testing**: Stable is thoroughly tested, reducing surprises during updates. Edge, as the continuously evolving branch, requires administrators to anticipate and manage compatibility challenges proactively.

- **Use Case Alignment**: Edge suits development, testing, and experimental contexts. Stable aligns well with production systems, embedded deployments, or scenarios demanding minimal operational risk.

The branching model of Alpine Linux pragmatically balances innovation and stability. It bestows administrators with the flexibility to tailor system behavior precisely to their requirements, whether that be bleeding-edge agility or long-term production-grade reliability. Understanding these nuances is essential for optimizing Alpine deployments and maintaining operational excellence.

1.5. Role in Containers and Security Ecosystems

Alpine Linux's emergence as a dominant force in container technology represents a confluence of factors centered around minimalism, security, and community-driven ecosystem support. Initially engineered as a general-purpose security-oriented distribution, Alpine's design principles have naturally aligned with the demands of modern containerized environments, where efficiency and risk reduction are paramount.

The defining characteristic that propelled Alpine Linux to prominence in containerization is its exceptionally small footprint. At approximately 5 MB for a base image, Alpine stands in marked contrast to traditional Linux distributions, which often exceed several hundred megabytes. This size advantage translates into faster deployment times, reduced bandwidth consumption in continuous integration pipelines, and lower storage requirements across registry and runtime infrastructures. Such compactness derives from Alpine's use of the musl libc implementation and BusyBox utilities, both designed to minimize resource overhead while providing essential Linux functionality. The importance of this minimalism is amplified in microservices architectures where containers are ephemeral and typically instantiated as lightweight atomic units, serving narrowly defined functions. Alpine's tiny base image thus facilitates rapid scalability and smoother orchestration by container runtimes.

Security considerations are intrinsic to Alpine's architecture, making it especially appealing to DevOps teams focused on robust production deployments.

21

The distribution employs Mandatory Access Control (MAC) via grsecurity patches (historically, although full grsecurity availability has fluctuated), hardened kernel defaults, and position-independent executables (PIE) compiled with stack-smashing protection, memory corruption mitigations, and fortification levels of compilation flags by default. These measures effectively harden the attack surface within container images, mitigating risks that commonly afflict containerized applications such as privilege escalations, arbitrary code execution, and binary tampering. Moreover, Alpine's package manager, apk, is streamlined for simplicity yet provides a curated set of packages minimizing transitive dependencies, which further constrains the risk of vulnerabilities introduced through excessive and unnecessary software bloat. Regular security audit practices supported by the Alpine community contribute to rapid patching and transparency, enabling swift adaptation to emerging threat vectors.

Within the expansive container ecosystem, Alpine has become the de facto base image for numerous official Docker images and microservices frameworks. Its adoption is visible in a wide range of language runtimes and application stacks-ranging from Python and Node.js to Go and Java distributions tailored for container environments. The Kubernetes ecosystem and Continuous Integration/Continuous Deployment (CI/CD) tooling chains benefit from Alpine's integration by providing consistent, lightweight starting points, allowing developers and operators to layer application-specific dependencies while minimizing upstream security and performance concerns. Alpine's compatibility with container orchestration tools further enhances its utility: its minimalism enables rapid container creation and destruction cycles, critical to scaling out stateless services in cloud-native deployments.

Another pivotal element in Alpine's container ecosystem integration is the ecosystem of Alpine-based official and community-maintained container images. This robust repository of images ensures that most services and utilities have Alpine equivalents optimized for security and size. Organizations leverage these Alpine-derived images to comply with best practices such as the principle of least privilege, where containers contain only the necessary components to function, thereby limiting exposure and simplifying compliance audits. Alpine's commitment to upstream package stability and predictable dependency resolution simplifies reproducible builds, an essential factor in maintaining secure supply chains in DevOps pipelines.

The synergy between Alpine Linux and container security extends to its interactions with runtime security frameworks and scanning tools. Modern container security platforms integrate Alpine's metadata and vulnerability feeds to provide enhanced visibility. Given Alpine's reduced attack surface, vulnerability scanning tools report fewer high-severity issues, leading to more manageable threat remediation workflows. This harmonization is crucial as container supply chains grow increasingly complex, with multiple layers of base images, application runtimes, and libraries, each presenting potential vulnerabilities. Alpine's disciplined approach to minimalism and security translates to container images that serve as more auditable and resilient foundations.

Despite its advantages, Alpine Linux in containers is not devoid of certain tradeoffs. The use of musl libc instead of GNU libc can lead to compatibility issues with pre-compiled binaries expecting glibc interfaces, necessitating careful dependency management. However, in security-sensitive environments, this distinction often serves as an additional barrier to arbitrary binary execution exploits and memory corruption, aligning with hardened security postures. Consequently, DevOps teams adopting Alpine often engage in meticulous application testing within containers to ensure functional integrity without sacrificing the security or size benefits.

In sum, Alpine Linux's meteoric rise within the container and security ecosystems is grounded in its unique blend of minimalism, fortified security mechanisms, and growing ecosystem support. This combination addresses three critical objectives in containerized deployments: reducing image size to enhance operational efficiency, imposing strict security hardening to minimize risks, and providing a well-supported platform enabling agile, secure software delivery. As containerization paradigms evolve with increasing complexity and scale, Alpine's role as a trusted foundation for secure microservices remains integral to the ongoing refinement of agile DevOps practices.

1.6. Community, Governance, and Support

Alpine Linux embodies a distinctive open governance model that is pivotal to its sustained innovation and robustness. Unlike centralized, hierarchical governance structures adopted by many distributions, Alpine employs a decentralized yet coordinated framework. This approach carefully balances meritocracy with inclusivity, fostering a community wherein contributions are rigorously evaluated, but accessibility for new developers and users remains paramount.

At the core of Alpine's governance is the *Alpine Development Team*, composed of trusted contributors who have demonstrated substantial expertise and commitment. Membership in this team is attained organically, primarily through sustained contributions to packaging, bug fixing, and documentation. Decision-making responsibilities, including approving new packages, managing repository branches, and coordinating releases, reside predominantly within this team. However, transparency is ensured by publicly accessible mailing lists and version control repositories, where all proposals and discussions occur openly. This public discourse mechanism permits not only Alpine developers but also the broader user community to observe, critique, and contribute to development dialogues.

In terms of development workflows, Alpine Linux adopts a streamlined Git-based process hosted on public platforms such as GitLab. Contributors submit changes through merge requests that undergo peer review by other team members. This review process prioritizes code quality, security considerations, and adherence to Alpine's minimalistic design philosophy. The lightweight musl libc and busybox core of Alpine enforce additional constraints that reviewers verify carefully, ensuring that package additions or updates do not compromise the system's goals: small size, simplicity, and security.

Workflow automation tooling plays a crucial role in maintaining code integrity and accelerating development cycles. Continuous integration pipelines automatically build and test packages against Alpine's supported architectures, verifying compliance with policies and triggering alerts on failures. This automation supports rapid iteration without sacrificing reliability or stability, a critical feature given Alpine's popularity in security-sensitive environments such as container orchestration.

Community engagement extends beyond the development team through multiple support and collaboration channels. The Alpine mailing list remains the primary forum for discussions ranging from user support to development announcements. These lists, archived and searchable, provide a rich knowledge repository and facilitate asynchronous communication accommodating global participation. IRC channels and modern chat platforms like Matrix supplement mailing lists, delivering real-time interaction opportunities. These venues enable immediate troubleshooting, mentoring, and exchange of best practices among novice and veteran Alpine users alike.

The Alpine wiki and official documentation are collaboratively maintained, incorporating contributions not only from core developers but also from a wide spectrum of users. This collective curatorial effort ensures that documentation evolves with the distribution and captures diverse use cases and deployment scenarios, including embedded systems, container deployments, and cloud-native infrastructures. Moderators and core developers regularly update policy documents within the repositories, including security advisories and package maintenance guidelines, keeping the information current and reliable.

An essential facet of Alpine's community ethos is its commitment to open, transparent governance that encourages leadership by merit and fosters innovation through collaboration. Proposals for significant changes, such as modifying default configurations or introducing new subsystems, undergo community-wide consultation prior to approval, reflecting a culture of consensus-building rather than unilateral decision-making. This approach balances agility with prudence, enabling Alpine to adapt swiftly in the dynamic open source ecosystem while safeguarding stability.

Long-term sustainability is further promoted by Alpine's permissive licensing model and the use of free software tools and libraries, which facilitate downstream adoption and integration. The distribution's modular architecture allows users and organizations to fork or customize Alpine without legal or technical barriers, potentially feeding improvements back upstream to the collective benefit. This reciprocal flow of innovation is reinforced by Alpine's participation in wider Linux and open source events, encouraging cross-pollination with adjacent projects and communities.

Alpine Linux's well-structured open governance and collaborative community environment underpin its continued success. By coupling rigorous development workflows and transparent decision processes with a vibrant network of support channels, Alpine not only nurtures innovation but also ensures resilience and adaptability. These attributes are essential for a distribution that targets cutting-edge deployment scenarios demanding both minimal footprints and uncompromising security. The Alpine model exemplifies how openness, meritocracy, and community engagement can coalesce to sustain a specialized Linux distribution capable of evolving alongside emerging technological paradigms.

Chapter 2

Installation Techniques and Deployment Models

The versatility of Alpine Linux truly shines when you explore its diverse installation methods and deployment topologies. Whether you're architecting a fleet of fire-and-forget embedded devices, orchestrating high-availability cloud infrastructure, or automating efficient diskless systems, this chapter reveals the tools and techniques that make Alpine uniquely adaptable. Uncover best practices as well as hidden challenges— learning to choose and optimize the right deployment strategy for any scenario.

2.1. Standard and Network-Based Installation

Alpine Linux, known for its minimalism and security focus, can be deployed through diverse installation methods tailored to different environments and scales. These methods primarily encompass installation from ISO images, bootable USB media, network-based PXE booting, and remote installation techniques, each offering unique advantages and practical considerations for rapid and reliable provisioning.

The standard installation approach uses downloadable ISO images, which are compact, hybrid disk images designed to be written onto various media. These ISO images can be used for direct installation on physical hardware or as virtual machines in hypervisor environments.

The installation process from an ISO image typically involves writing the image to a bootable medium (CD/DVD or USB) or directly booting the ISO in virtualization software. Upon boot, the Alpine setup scripts provide an interactive command-line interface that guides through disk partitioning, package selection, and network configuration.

Advantages:

- *Simplicity*: The process is straightforward with minimal prerequisites.

- *Flexibility*: Suitable for single machines or small-scale deployments without specialized infrastructure.

- *Quick boot*: The ISO is designed for fast startup and minimal memory use.

Disadvantages:

- *Manual intervention*: Requires user interaction, which limits automation.

- *Limited scalability*: Not ideal for provisioning large numbers of systems efficiently.

The ISO image can be downloaded from the official Alpine Linux repository. After writing the image to USB media using utilities like dd or Rufus, the system boots into the Alpine installer with the following automatic shell prompt:

```
setup-alpine
```

This script leads the installer through configuration steps, for example, selecting the keyboard layout, setting up networking through DHCP or static IP, and partitioning disks with fdisk or parted. Installation concludes with package installation and configuration of the bootloader.

Using USB devices as boot media is nearly identical in process to ISO booting but offers enhanced portability and ease of use. The ISO image is transferred onto a USB stick using command-line tools or graphical utilities, rendering it bootable.

Advantages:

- *Portability*: USB sticks are compact, reusable, and widely supported by modern hardware.

- *Speed*: Typically faster boot times compared to optical media.

- *Convenience*: Easy to update or modify installation media.

Disadvantages:

- *Compatibility*: Some systems, especially older ones, might not support USB boot.

- *Wear*: USB flash drives have limited write cycles, potentially reducing longevity if used repeatedly.

Creating USB media can be performed as follows:

```
# Example command to write Alpine ISO to a USB device
dd if=alpine-standard-3.18.2-x86_64.iso of=/dev/sdX bs=4
    M status=progress && sync
```

Replace /dev/sdX with the appropriate device identifier. After writing, the USB must be properly ejected to ensure data integrity.

Preboot Execution Environment (PXE) booting leverages network infrastructure to initiate an Alpine Linux installation without local boot media. PXE enables systems to load a minimal kernel and initramfs over the network, facilitating automated, reproducible installations at scale.

The PXE boot process involves a DHCP server to provide network parameters and a TFTP server to serve boot files. The client obtains IP configuration and the location of the boot loader and kernel via DHCP options, then downloads these components over TFTP to start the installer.

Advantages:

- *Scalability*: Ideal for deploying Alpine Linux across numerous machines simultaneously.

- *Automation*: Can be integrated with configuration management and provisioning tools.

- *No physical media*: Eliminates the need for flash drives or optical disks.

Disadvantages:

- *Infrastructure dependency*: Requires a functional DHCP and TFTP setup, which may complicate initial setup.

- *Network speed and reliability*: Installation speed depends on network performance.

A minimal PXE setup for Alpine involves preparing the following:

- **TFTP server**: Hosting the Alpine kernel and initramfs files.

- **DHCP server configuration**: Providing the PXE boot menu and paths to TFTP files via DHCP options 66 and 67 or using proxy DHCP.

The PXE bootloader configuration includes kernel parameters specifying the root filesystem and networking options for an automated setup or interactive installer launch.

Beyond PXE, remote installation techniques take advantage of network protocols for deploying Alpine Linux on physically inaccessible or virtualized hosts. Common methods incorporate:

- **SSH-based installation**: After booting from minimal media (like an initramfs), Alpine can be installed and configured remotely over SSH, allowing direct command-line control.

- **Preseed/Automation scripts**: Alpine supports script-driven installations via `alpine-conf`, enabling automated system setup when combined with network file shares or HTTP serving installation scripts.

- **Cloud-init and container-oriented installs**: Alpine integrates well in cloud and containerized environments where provisioning is managed via cloud-init meta-data or container orchestration systems.

Advantages:

- *Automation potential*: Enables fully unattended installations, reducing human error and accelerating deployment.

- *Access to headless systems*: Particularly valuable for servers lacking direct console access.

Disadvantages:

- *Complexity*: Requires careful scripting and network setup.

- *Security considerations*: Remote access must be secured, typically via SSH keys and firewall rules.

Example of using SSH to perform remote setup once minimal Alpine boot media is initiated:

```
ssh root@target-ip
setup-alpine
exit
reboot
```

This approach assumes the target system has network connectivity and SSH enabled in the initial ramdisk environment.

Each installation method serves particular deployment scenarios:

Method	Ease of Setup	Automation	Scalability	Hardware Requirements
ISO Image	High	Low	Low	Individual local or VM access
USB Media	High	Low	Low	USB boot capable hardware
PXE Boot	Medium	High	High	Network infrastructure capable of PXE
Remote Installations	Low	Very High	Very High	Network + SSH access

For single-node or small deployments, ISO and USB-based installations remain practical due to their simplicity and direct control. Conversely, network-based methods—PXE and remote scripted installation—excel in cloud, data center, or lab environments demanding rapid, repeatable provisioning on numerous machines.

Combining PXE with automation scripts kickstarted by Alpine's `setup-alpine` utility can reduce human input while maintaining customizability. Provisioning pipelines often incorporate configuration management tools like Ansible or SaltStack to finalize installation and post-configuration, enhancing reproducibility and compliance.

In all circumstances, meticulous preparation of boot media or network services, robust testing in staging environments, and clear documentation of installation workflows are essential to secure consistent, dependable system deployment at scale.

35

2.2. Diskless and Data Disk Modes

Alpine Linux introduces a versatile installation framework that extends beyond the traditional persistent sys model, offering two distinct paradigms: the diskless (RAM-resident) mode and the data disk mode. These alternative modes cater to diverse deployment scenarios where the conventional approach either imposes constraints or fails to optimally utilize the system's capabilities. Understanding these modes requires delineating their operational principles, deployment use cases, and trade-offs in comparison to the standard persistent installation.

The *diskless* mode centers on loading the entire operating system into a volatile memory space, typically RAM, at boot time. Under this mode, Alpine is installed or copied onto a medium used solely for initial bootstrapping, such as a USB drive or network disk. Once the kernel and initial ramdisk initialize, the root filesystem is mounted as a tmpfs-a temporary filesystem that resides entirely in memory. This approach effectively renders the system stateless with respect to persistent disk storage, as all modifications to the filesystem occur in RAM and disappear upon reboot unless explicitly saved externally.

The diskless mode, often termed RAM-resident, suits deployments requiring ephemeral sessions or environments where data integrity after power cycles is unnecessary or undesirable. Common scenarios include live demonstration systems, unattended kiosks, or security-hardened environments where write-once, read-many operation prevents host contamination. This mode provides exceptionally fast runtime performance for file operations, as RAM access times significantly outperform physical storage media, though it is limited by the available system memory.

Interaction with persistent storage in diskless systems is generally mediated through network shares or dedicated data volumes mounted independently of the root filesystem. Alpine's modular design and its initialization scripts facilitate early mounting of such storage targets, allowing user and application data to persist separately while the system root remains transient. This separation enhances system resilience against disk failure and simplifies upgrades, as the kernel and base system may be seamlessly refreshed without impacting user data. Nonetheless, a well-constructed backup strategy must accompany diskless use to protect critical information residing outside the ephemeral root.

In contrast, the *data disk* mode adopts a hybrid configuration: Alpine's operating system files remain on a persistent root filesystem, while user data and frequently modified files reside on separate dedicated partitions or disks. The fundamental distinction from a pure sys install lies in the explicit segregation and management of data and system volumes. This mode ensures that routine data writes do not affect system partition integrity, which can be mounted read-only or maintained with higher redundancy measures such as RAID. Such partitioning is invaluable in environments emphasizing data integrity and system stability, including database servers, enterprise appliances, and embedded systems.

System-level updates in data disk mode minimize downtime because they can be performed on the system volume independently, facilitating rollback and snapshotting techniques without risking user data loss. Additionally, the clear separation allows optimized backup schemes and simplifies compliance with data protection policies. Configuration management tools integrated within the Alpine ecosystem leverage this architecture to apply updates or system changes selectively.

The conventional sys mode remains relevant for scenarios demanding a straightforward installation with full read-write capabilities on a single root filesystem. It benefits environments where system persistence, ease of mainte-nance, and compatibility with traditional Linux workflows are paramount. However, this model is susceptible to in-creased boot times due to disk I/O and carries a larger se-curity risk surface when both system and data reside to-gether, potentially exacerbating the impact of corruption or unauthorized modifications.

Selecting the appropriate mode-diskless, data disk, or sys-hinges on operational objectives and hardware con-straints. Diskless installations excel when immutability and rapid restoration are critical. This mode is often de-ployed in virtualized or containerized environments to maximize hardware utilization and facilitate rapid cloning. Conversely, data disk mode is selected in high-availability deployments requiring fault tolerance and performance optimization through storage tiering. The sys model suits conventional use cases demanding simplicity and adapt-ability.

The complexity of each mode also influences orchestra-tion and monitoring strategies. Diskless nodes, by virtue of their transient nature, often require external environ-ments for logging, configuration persistence, and appli-cation state management. Data disk mode installations generally leverage standard Linux tools for filesystem in-tegrity and snapshot management, while persistent sys installations benefit from the broad ecosystem of package management and system recovery utilities.

Overall, Alpine's flexible installation modes embody an architectural philosophy prioritizing minimalism, configurability, and resilience. Through careful alignment of mode selection with deployment characteristics-ranging from stateless live systems to robust data-centric servers-administrators can tailor the operating system to exacting technical requirements. This adaptability positions Alpine as an ideal choice across cloud-native applications, embedded systems, and specialized appliances, each deriving distinct benefits from the interplay of diskless and data disk paradigms alongside the conventional persistent model.

2.3. Custom Partitioning and Filesystem Layouts

Advanced partitioning and filesystem layout strategies enable system architects and administrators to optimize storage configurations tailored to specific performance goals, security requirements, and hardware environments. These techniques extend beyond basic partitioning, incorporating flexible automation and diverse filesystem choices to address varying workloads and deployment contexts, including modern cloud infrastructures and heterogeneous hardware platforms.

Partitioning schemes fundamentally impact how data is stored, accessed, and maintained. Custom partitioning begins with a clear understanding of system use cases, such as database servers requiring high I/O throughput, embedded devices constrained by flash memory wear, or cloud instances demanding rapid scalability and security isolation. Partition sizes, alignment, and type decisions must be made with careful consideration of these factors, often at an interactive level via tools like `parted` or `gdisk`, or through scripted mechanisms to ensure repeatability across multiple environments.

39

Automated partitioning scripts leverage utilities such as sgdisk for GPT partitioning or sfdisk for MBR systems, enabling predefined layouts that can be version-controlled and dynamically adjusted. Example shell commands can be embedded within deployment scripts to finalize partition arrangements before filesystems are created and mounted:

```
#!/bin/bash
DEVICE=/dev/sdx
# Clear existing partition table
sgdisk --zap-all $DEVICE
# Create EFI System Partition (ESP)
sgdisk --new=1:2048:+512M --typecode=1:ef00 --change-
    name=1:'EFI System' $DEVICE
# Create Linux root partition
sgdisk --new=2:0:+20G --typecode=2:8300 --change-name
    =2:'Root Filesystem' $DEVICE
# Create Linux data partition
sgdisk --new=3:0:0 --typecode=3:8300 --change-name=3:'
    Data Partition' $DEVICE
```

Filesystem selection is closely coupled with the partition layout to leverage performance characteristics and management features suited to the workload. Common filesystems such as ext4 balance maturity and performance; however, specialized options like XFS, Btrfs, or ZFS introduce benefits like scalable metadata handling, built-in snapshotting, and integrated checksumming.

- XFS excels in large-scale data environments due to its efficient allocation group structure and delayed allocation, which mitigates fragmentation. Its scalability is beneficial in cloud-native storage systems where dynamic resizing and rapid metadata updates are common.

- Btrfs supports flexible snapshot and subvolume management, which simplifies backup workflows and lifecycle operations but may have complex tuning requirements to optimize performance.

40

Lifecycle management involves planning for data integrity, backup, and system recovery. Filesystems offering native snapshot capabilities reduce downtime by enabling point-in-time copies with minimal resource impact. Additionally, partitioning schemes can separate system, application, and user data partitions, allowing independent backup and reinstallation processes without data loss or extended outages.

Security considerations influence both partitioning and filesystem choices. Partition-level encryption via LUKS or hardware-based options such as TPM-bound volumes provide fundamental data confidentiality. Combining encrypted partitions with filesystems that support access control lists (ACLs) or extended attributes (xattr) enables fine-grained permission policies tailored to multi-tenant cloud environments or compliance-intensive workloads.

In virtualized and cloud architectures, ephemeral storage often utilizes a layered approach, where a base read-only image is overlaid by writable snapshots or ephemeral partitions. Automated partitioning scripts can include preparation for such configurations, enabling fast instance spin-up and teardown, while filesystem choices support the transient nature of these storage layers.

Performance tuning of filesystems within custom partitions utilizes mount options and kernel parameters that control caching behavior, journaling modes, and write ordering. For instance, ext4 can be mounted with data=writeback to maximize throughput at the cost of stronger crash consistency guarantees, whereas Btrfs can be tuned by adjusting the commit interval or disabling checksum verification on certain datasets to reduce overhead.

Hardware-specific considerations are crucial. On SSDs,

partition alignment to erase block sizes and filesystem queue depth settings mitigate write amplification and prolong device lifespan. Filesystems like F2FS target flash storage explicitly, optimizing for wear-leveling and garbage collection. For high-performance NVMe devices, combining RAID configurations with carefully tuned filesystems can produce balanced throughput and resilience.

Ultimately, a holistic approach to custom partitioning and filesystem layouts harmonizes system requirements, hardware characteristics, and operational constraints. Automated tooling and scripting preserve consistency and reduce human error, while interactive tools provide flexibility during exploratory or unique configurations. Selecting appropriate filesystems aligned with these partitioning strategies enhances system performance, security, and maintainability across a broad spectrum of technological environments.

2.4. Automated and Headless Deployments

Automated and headless deployments represent foundational techniques for scaling infrastructure provisioning, enabling managed, repeatable, and unattended installation processes. This paradigm shifts traditional manual intervention to a reproducible, script-driven approach, resolving challenges that arise from complex environments such as large server farms, geographically dispersed edge devices, or continuous integration (CI) testbeds. Core to this practice is the concept of configuration automation, achieved through pre-seeding and provisioning mechanisms that eliminate the need for human interaction during installation.

The essential characteristic of automated deployment is the ability to specify, in advance, all installation parameters and post-installation configurations. This is often realized through pre-seeding files or analogous configuration descriptors, which define variables such as partitioning schemes, network interfaces, package selections, user accounts, security policies, and system services. These configuration files serve as declarative blueprints for the operating system installer or configuration management system, ensuring that each deployment instance aligns precisely with organizational standards.

Consider, for example, Debian-based systems that support the preseed mechanism. A preseed.cfg file may contain directives specifying disk partitioning:

```
d-i partman-auto/method string lvm
d-i partman-auto-lvm/guided_size string max
d-i partman-auto/choose_recipe select atomic
d-i partman/confirm_write_new_label boolean true
d-i partman/confirm boolean true
```

The installer consumes this input without halting for manual selections, orchestrating disk preparation dynamically. Analogously, Red Hat and derivatives utilize Kickstart files (ks.cfg), which incorporate scripted installation instructions with agility comparable to preseeding. A Kickstart excerpt that automates network configuration might appear as follows:

```
network --bootproto=dhcp --device=eth0 --onboot=yes --
    ipv6=auto
rootpw --plaintext securepassword
firewall --enabled --http --ssh
```

Automated deployments are often augmented with provisioning scripts executed after the base system installation completes. These scripts, frequently written in shell,

Python, or another scripting language, handle system customization tasks including software installation, configuration file templating, and service orchestration. Such scripts may be invoked via installer hooks or configuration management agents, leveraging tools like `cloud-init` for cloud environments or `Ansible`, `Puppet`, and `Chef` for both initial bootstrapping and ongoing orchestration.

An example bash provisioning script that configures essential services after base install might be:

```
#!/bin/bash
apt-get update
apt-get install -y nginx mysql-server
systemctl enable nginx
systemctl start nginx
mysql_secure_installation <<EOF

y
new_password
new_password
y
y
y
y
EOF
```

Automated deployment workflows benefit significantly from integration within Continuous Integration and Continuous Deployment (CI/CD) pipelines. Infrastructure as Code (IaC) principles guide the management of deployment configurations and provisioning scripts within source control, enabling automated testing and iterative refinement. Techniques such as immutable infrastructure and containerization further supplement automated deployments by encapsulating environments, reducing configuration drift, and simplifying rollback procedures.

Headless deployment environments-systems without graphical user interfaces or direct human access-require special consideration. Network booting technologies

44

like PXE (Preboot Execution Environment) serve as pivotal enablers, allowing bare-metal hosts or devices to boot the installer directly from network resources. When combined with a curated preseed or Kickstart configuration, PXE-based deployments facilitate rapid, consistent provisioning across large fleets without physical interaction. The typical PXE boot cycle involves DHCP and TFTP servers distributing network parameters and bootloaders, which then fetch installer kernels and initramfs images, executing installation autonomously.

The architecture of fully automated deployments often incorporates the following components:

- **Bootstrap Infrastructure:** DHCP, TFTP, HTTP, and other servers providing network boot services and installation media.

- **Configuration Artifacts:** Preseed, Kickstart, or analogous files defining installation parameters.

- **Provisioning Scripts:** Custom scripts to finalize system setup beyond the installer's scope.

- **Configuration Management:** Tools for maintaining system state post-deployment.

- **Orchestration Pipelines:** CI/CD frameworks managing deployment lifecycle and validation.

The compounded effect of automation is heightened reliability and speed across deployments. Manual configuration errors diminish as installations become repeatable processes driven by controlled inputs. Moreover, automated deployments support heterogeneous hardware environments and multi-tenant infrastructures by codifying variability into parameterized configuration files and modular scripts.

Careful development and validation of automation artifacts are paramount. Due to the lack of interactive installers, misconfigurations can result in silent failures or incomplete setups. It is prudent to employ iterative testing via virtual machines or staging environments before widespread rollout. Logging and failure recovery mechanisms should also be embedded within provisioning phases to facilitate troubleshooting.

In distributed or remote device scenarios-such as Internet of Things (IoT) nodes or edge compute servers-headless and automated deployments enable seamless updates and scaling. Systems can be mass-reprovisioned remotely, supporting rapid iteration of software payloads or kernel upgrades with minimal operational overhead.

In essence, automated and headless deployment methodologies transform infrastructure provisioning into a deterministic, programmable activity. By leveraging pre-seeding frameworks and scripting automation, organizations can achieve scalability, consistency, and agility essential for modern computing environments. This paradigm not only reduces operational costs but also lays the groundwork for advanced infrastructure lifecycle management and full DevOps integration.

2.5. Cloud Platform Integration

Alpine Linux has established itself as a minimalistic, security-oriented distribution favored for cloud deployments, and its integration with major cloud platforms is facilitated by a suite of pre-built images and automation tools. These images are tailored to leverage each cloud provider's infrastructure optimally, providing a consistent foundation while allowing flexibility for customization and scaling. This section delves into the availability of Alpine images across prominent cloud providers: Amazon Web Services (AWS), Google Cloud Platform (GCP), Microsoft Azure, and OpenStack, and highlights the cloud-init framework as a pivotal component for automated instance configuration. It further discusses best practices for deploying and managing Alpine instances in both public and private cloud environments.

Pre-built Alpine Images on Cloud Providers

Cloud providers typically offer official or community-supported Alpine Linux images as part of their marketplace or public image catalogs. These images are crafted to comply with each platform's specific requirements for instance initialization, storage, and networking.

- **Amazon Web Services (AWS):**
  AWS provides Alpine images in multiple regions through the Amazon Machine Image (AMI) system. These AMIs are maintained to align with the latest Alpine stable releases, incorporating configuration tuned for AWS's EC2 environment, such as optimized cloud-init integration and kernel modules compatible with the AWS Nitro system. Users can access these images via the AWS Marketplace or by specifying the appropriate AMI ID in deployment scripts.

- **Google Cloud Platform (GCP):**
  GCP hosts Alpine images in its Cloud Marketplace and the public image repository. The images are configured to interact seamlessly with Google Cloud's metadata service for instance metadata retrieval and support the use of Google's OS Config management

47

tools. The minimal footprint of Alpine results in faster boot times and reduced attack surfaces compared to larger distributions.

- **Microsoft Azure:**
  Azure supports Alpine Linux through Marketplace images that have been adapted for Hyper-V virtual hardware and Azure's managed storage systems. These images are equipped with Azure-specific cloud-init modules enabling integration with Azure Resource Manager (ARM) templates and Azure VM extensions.

- **OpenStack:**
  OpenStack users can utilize Alpine images that conform to standard image formats such as qcow2. Alpine's compatibility with OpenStack's metadata service and support for cloud-init make it an excellent choice for private cloud deployments. Community-maintained images are updated regularly and validated for performance within typical OpenStack setups.

Cloud-init: Automated Configuration and Initialization

Cloud-init is a widely adopted framework that automates the initialization and configuration of cloud instances during the first boot. Alpine Linux supports cloud-init to enable dynamic setup without manual intervention, essential for scalable and repeatable deployment pipelines.

When an Alpine instance boots, cloud-init executes user data scripts or configuration directives retrieved from the cloud provider's metadata service. This enables a variety of tasks, including:

- Network configuration, including assignment of IP addresses and routing.

- User account creation with SSH key injection for secure access.

- Package installation and service restarts.

- Execution of configuration management client agents.

Cloud-init configuration is typically provided in YAML format, allowing declarative setup. For Alpine, it is important to verify that the installed cloud-init version matches the capabilities expected by the cloud platform's metadata service, as discrepancies can lead to deployment errors.

```
#cloud-config
hostname: alpine-cloud-instance
users:
  - default
  - name: admin
    ssh-authorized-keys:
      - ssh-rsa AAAAB3NzaC1yc2...
    sudo: ['ALL=(ALL) NOPASSWD:ALL']
    shell: /bin/ash
packages:
  - curl
  - htop
runcmd:
  - systemctl enable sshd
  - systemctl start sshd
```

Best Practices for Deploying Alpine in Cloud Environments

Deploying Alpine Linux in cloud environments requires adherence to best practices that ensure security, performance, and ease of management.

- **Image Selection and Customization:**
  While pre-built Alpine images provide a solid baseline, custom images tailored to organizational re-

quirements can improve deployment efficiency. Employing configuration management tools such as Ansible or Terraform in conjunction with cloud-init allows for immutable infrastructure models where Alpine instances are ephemeral and fully configured upon launch.

- **Security Considerations:**
Alpine's minimal attack surface combined with frequent security patching is suitable for hardened environments. It is crucial to enable encrypted volumes where supported by the cloud provider and restrict network access using security groups or firewall rules. Additionally, disabling unnecessary services and employing SSH key-based authentication limits exposure.

- **Resource Optimization:**
Due to its lightweight nature, Alpine excels in minimizing resource consumption. When deploying in cloud environments with pay-as-you-go pricing, right-sizing instances and using Alpine can lead to cost savings. It is advisable to monitor resource usage and adjust instance types dynamically via auto-scaling groups tied to workload demand.

- **Integration with Cloud-specific Features:**
Leveraging metadata services, custom tags, and cloud provider APIs enhances orchestration. For example, in AWS, integration with Elastic Load Balancers (ELBs) and Amazon CloudWatch for logging and metrics can facilitate high availability and observability of Alpine-based workloads.

- **Usage in Private Clouds:**
For private cloud environments managed via OpenStack or similar platforms, Alpine images offer con-

sistent performance and ease of integration. Automation tools like MaaS (Metal as a Service) combined with cloud-init can streamline bare-metal provisioning of Alpine, supporting hybrid cloud strategies effectively.

Management and Maintenance

Ongoing management of Alpine instances in cloud settings benefits from automated patching and consistent configuration validation using desired state configuration paradigms. Regular updates of base images and avoiding manual modifications on running instances reduce configuration drift. Container orchestration platforms, such as Kubernetes, can further abstract the management by running Alpine as a container base image, benefitting from the same minimalism and security focus in clustered deployments.

The availability of pre-built Alpine images in major cloud providers coupled with cloud-init's automation capabilities supports agile, secure, and efficient deployment practices. Adopting best practices in configuration, security, and resource management is pivotal to fully harnessing Alpine Linux in modern cloud ecosystems, whether public or private.

2.6. Firmware and Secure Boot Considerations

The firmware interface fundamentally governs the initialization of computing platforms, influencing the boot process, platform security, and hardware compatibility. Two dominant firmware paradigms, Unified Extensible Firmware Interface (UEFI) and legacy Basic Input/Output System (BIOS), coexist in contemporary server environments, each carrying distinct operational and security characteristics that must be carefully navigated to ensure robust and secure system deployment.

UEFI, designed as a modern replacement for legacy BIOS, provides a more flexible and extensible environment for platform initialization. It supports larger boot volumes, pre-boot applications, and a modular driver model. Critically, UEFI incorporates Secure Boot, a security feature that enforces cryptographic validation of bootloaders and firmware drivers before execution, thereby mitigating the risk of boot-level malware or rootkits. Secure Boot leverages a public key infrastructure embedded within firmware, allowing only signed and trusted binaries to execute, which enhances the chain of trust from platform power-on to operating system loading.

Legacy BIOS, though lacking native Secure Boot capabilities, remains prevalent in older hardware platforms and some specialized systems. BIOS systems perform initialization and locate a bootloader in the Master Boot Record (MBR) without cryptographic verification, rendering them vulnerable to bootkits and unauthorized firmware modifications. This absence of secure boot validation mandates complementary or compensatory security measures, such as employing hardware root-of-trust anchors, integrating trusted platform modules (TPMs), or utilizing runtime attestation mechanisms.

Transitioning between these firmware technologies introduces notable operational challenges. Primarily, hardware compatibility is a critical concern: certain legacy devices or peripherals may lack appropriate UEFI drivers or support, constraining the server's ability to fully harness UEFI features. Conversely, modern hardware increasingly favors UEFI for enabling advanced functionality and security features, compelling environments with legacy BIOS to undertake careful hardware evaluation or employ hybrid boot strategies during migration.

Effective deployment strategies must reconcile these firmware nuances. For servers with UEFI firmware, enabling Secure Boot should be undertaken with attention to key management and platform configuration. Integration of custom Platform Key (PK), Key Exchange Keys (KEK), and signature databases (db and dbx) requires disciplined key lifecycle and update management processes, ensuring that authorized software components remain valid while revoked or compromised binaries are excluded. Additionally, organizations must consider firmware updates or Manufacturer-Supplied Keys (MSK), balancing out-of-the-box compatibility with security posture.

In legacy BIOS contexts, where Secure Boot is unavailable, mitigating boot-time risk often involves leveraging a hardware root of trust via TPMs to enable measured boot. Measured boot processes entail sequential hashing of firmware and boot components, storing measurements in Platform Configuration Registers (PCRs) that can be evaluated to detect unauthorized modifications. This approach complements software-based integrity checks and can integrate with remote attestation frameworks, providing assurance in environments where cryptographic boot verification is inherently unsupported.

Another practical consideration involves the bootloader itself. UEFI bootloaders typically utilize the EFI Sys-

53

tem Partition formatted with GPT, while BIOS-compatible systems rely on MBR layout. Deploying a unified image or multi-boot environment necessitates compatibility strategies such as dual bootloaders or hybrid partitioning schemes to accommodate disparate firmware expectations without compromising security. Automated deployment pipelines should incorporate firmware-aware validation steps to prevent boot failures or security policy violations arising from incompatibilities.

Hardware vendor documentation and community resources are invaluable for understanding firmware-specific nuances, including Secure Boot implementation details, BIOS customization options, and firmware update mechanisms. Rigorous firmware validation during system commissioning, including verifying Secure Boot states and measuring boot integrity, ensures alignment with organizational security requirements.

Balancing UEFI and legacy BIOS considerations requires a comprehensive understanding of their fundamental operational differences, security capabilities, and hardware ecosystem constraints. Securing the boot process in modern server infrastructures entails not only enabling Secure Boot where available but also implementing complementary cryptographic and attestation mechanisms on legacy platforms. Designing deployment strategies with firmware compatibility and security policies in concert ensures resilient and trustworthy platform initialization across heterogeneous server landscapes.

Chapter 3

Advanced Package Management and Customization

Beneath Alpine Linux's minimalist surface lies a finely-tuned system for managing software with surgical precision. This chapter is your key to mastering the unique apk package manager, engineering custom repositories, enforcing airtight security, and tailoring systems perfectly to your needs. Explore the often-overlooked mechanisms and strategies that transform software management from a chore into a robust, automated, and verifiable process, unlocking Alpine's full potential in enterprise production environments.

3.1. Mastering apk: Features and Internals

The apk package manager, integral to Alpine Linux, provides an efficient and minimalist approach to software management. Beyond its basic functionality of package installation and removal, apk encompasses sophisticated features designed to optimize dependency resolution, provide extensibility through scripting hooks, and facilitate troubleshooting in complex package scenarios. Mastery of these capabilities allows system administrators to harness apk's full potential both in everyday environments and large-scale deployments.

At the core of apk's operation lies its dependency resolution mechanism, which ensures that package installations preserve system consistency while minimizing redundant downloads and conflicts. When a package request is issued, apk evaluates the package's defined dependencies and recursively resolves them, taking into account the state of the installed package set. It does so efficiently by employing a lightweight dependency graph traversal combined with version constraint checking. Package constraints are expressed as a combination of operators such as >=, <, =, etc., accompanying package names to specify acceptable version ranges. For instance, the declaration

```
depends="libc>=0.7.0"
```

in a .APKBUILD script mandates installation or upgrade of libc to version 0.7.0 or higher. apk evaluates these dependencies against locally cached index files, which are compact SQLite databases containing package metadata fetched from remote repositories. This indexed approach accelerates lookups and allows apk to perform atomic transactions, thereby avoiding partial system states during upgrades or installations.

A compelling feature in apk for advanced use is the support for scripting hooks embedded in the package lifecycle. Maintainers can specify pre-install, post-install, pre-upgrade, and post-upgrade scripts within a package's control archive using shell scripts placed in predefined directories under usr/lib/apk/hooks/. These hooks facilitate customized configuration or cleanup procedures essential for complex software stacks. For example, a post-install script may perform service restarts or update kernel modules dynamically. The scripts execute under a controlled environment that provides critical environment variables such as APK_PACKAGE_NAME, APK_OLD_VERSION, and APK_NEW_VERSION, enabling context-aware operations.

```
#!/bin/sh
# post-install hook example
if [ "$APK_PACKAGE_NAME" = "nginx" ]; then
    rc-service nginx restart
fi
```

System administrators can also leverage apk's scripting capabilities to create extensions for operational automation, such as environment-specific configuration patching or conditional dependency installation, thus tailoring package behavior for diverse deployment scenarios.

For troubleshooting complex installations, apk provides verbose logging and query options designed to diagnose dependency conflicts, broken repositories, or corrupted package caches. The apk info -L command lists files installed by a package, useful for verifying file locations and detecting unintended file overwrites. The apk fix command allows repair of corrupted or partially installed packages by reinstallation from the repository without removing current configurations or data files.

57

Dependency conflicts can be examined with `apk audit`, which verifies the installed packages against known security vulnerabilities and dependency satisfactions. When facing repository synchronization issues, administrators can manually update the repository indexes using

```
apk update --no-cache
```

to force refresh without retaining local caches that may cause stale metadata resolution. This tactic is particularly effective in CI/CD pipelines or immutable system containers requiring fresh and consistent states for every build.

In large-scale environments, apk's low memory footprint and fast database operations enable integration with configuration management tools and automated orchestration systems. Scripts invoking `apk` can be chained or conditionalized within infrastructure-as-code frameworks, empowering reliable and repeatable system provisioning workflows. Moreover, apk's ability to lock package versions via pinning mechanisms prevents destabilizing upgrades in production, thus maintaining environment consistency.

The `apk` package manager also supports package repositories over HTTPS with signature verification using apk keys for cryptographic authenticity and integrity, a necessity in secure system administration. Repository keys can be manually managed or imported with:

```
apk add <package> --allow-untrusted
```

only when deliberately overriding verification policies, ensuring that accidental or malicious installations are minimized.

Unlocking the advanced functionalities of apk-dependency resolution strategies, lifecycle scripting hooks, and comprehensive troubleshooting commands-empowers system administrators to maintain lean, secure, and resilient Alpine Linux systems. By exploiting these features, administrators can efficiently manage both daily package operations and complex system upgrades in scalable, automated infrastructures.

3.2. Repository Management and Mirror Optimization

The orchestration of software repositories in large-scale environments demands a meticulous balance between availability, freshness, and performance. Managing both official and custom repositories necessitates not only strategic setup but continuous maintenance to assure data integrity and rapid delivery of packages to clients. A comprehensive approach to repository management involves effective mirror selection, synchronization strategies, and optimization techniques that enhance reliability and scalability.

Official repositories, typically maintained by upstream vendors or community projects, provide the foundational software packages for numerous applications. Custom repositories serve as augmented layers, hosting propri-etary or internally vetted packages. Both repository categories require robust lifecycle management that covers initialization, periodic updates, and validation to prevent pollution or inconsistencies.

Establishing a repository begins with defining its role (official or custom), specifying the storage architecture, and configuring access controls. The repository metadata, which indexes available packages, must be accurately generated and periodically refreshed using tools such as `createrepo` for RPM-based systems or dpkg-scanpackages for Debian-based systems. The repository configuration manifests include URL endpoints and GPG key integration to facilitate package signing verification during client-side transactions.

A critical step in repository deployment is selecting a storage backend optimized for read efficiency, since repositories predominantly serve binary packages rather than undergoing frequent write operations. Implementations often leverage network-attached storage (NAS) or distributed file systems with high throughput and low latency. When accommodating custom repositories, it is essential to maintain clear versioning and naming conventions to avoid conflicts with official packages.

Effective mirror selection is fundamental to achieving fault tolerance and load distribution. Hierarchical repository structures introduce local mirrors situated within organizational networks proximate to client nodes, reducing network latency and bandwidth consumption. Remote mirrors, typically located geographically closer to the end-users or in high-availability data centers, act as upstream sources for these local mirrors.

Mirror selection mechanisms encompass geographic-based routing, latency measurements, and reliability scoring. Systems such as DNS-based Global Server Load Balancing (GSLB) dynamically resolve repository URLs to the optimal mirror endpoint. Alternative approaches utilize content delivery networks (CDNs) to cache repository data at edge locations globally. For environments lacking commercial CDN services, a custom mesh of mirrors synchronized via robust synchronization methods often constitutes an efficient model.

Synchronization serves to keep mirrors current yet im-

poses challenges in handling large data volumes and minimizing inconsistency windows. Tools such as rsync remain the cornerstone for repository synchronization due
to their delta-transfer algorithms and resilience over un-
reliable networks.

Advanced synchronization strategies exploit metadata
repositories, where mirrors periodically fetch lightweight
metadata updates instead of complete repositories. This
differential sync significantly reduces bandwidth and
accelerates update propagation. For RPM repositories,
reposync provides automated downloads of new or
updated packages by interrogating repository metadata.

An illustrative rsync synchronization command is:

```
rsync -avz --delete rsync://mirror.example.org/repos/
    official/ /var/www/html/repos/official/
```

The --delete flag ensures removal of packages no
longer present upstream, maintaining mirror consistency.
Synchronization intervals are tuned to balance freshness
against resource consumption, with latency-sensitive
environments favoring near real-time updates.

Repository performance optimization hinges on caching
mechanisms, parallel data retrieval, and request throttling
policies. Implementing caching proxies such as Squid or
specialized package caching solutions like apt-cacher-ng
reduces redundant data transfers by intercepting package
requests and serving cached content to multiple clients.

Parallelizing synchronization jobs across multiple threads
or nodes can expedite initial mirror population or large updates. However, concurrency must be carefully managed
to avoid bandwidth saturation or repository database corruption.

Compression algorithms applied to repository metadata

and packages, such as gzip or xz, impact download speeds and storage requirements. Striking an optimal balance between compression ratio and decompression overhead is necessary, often influenced by client hardware capabilities.

Reliability is achieved through rigorous integrity verification using cryptographic signatures at both metadata and package levels. Continuous health monitoring of mirror servers, automated failover mechanisms, and alerting systems collectively contribute to operational stability.

Scalability encompasses horizontal scaling via additional mirror nodes and load balancing layers, accommodating increased user demands without degrading performance. Containerization and orchestration platforms can assist in deploying scalable mirror infrastructures rapidly with consistent configuration.

In extensive deployments, a federated repository architecture can be established, whereby multiple organizational units manage dedicated mirrors synchronized in a mesh topology, improving redundancy and responsiveness.

- Implement clearly defined repository roles and maintain consistent versioning schemes to prevent package conflicts.

- Utilize geographically optimal mirrors with DNS-based routing or CDN integration for efficient client access.

- Employ incremental synchronization strategies augmented by metadata differencing to minimize bandwidth and keep repositories current.

- Introduce caching proxies and parallel synchronization to enhance data availability and reduce load.

- Integrate verification mechanisms and monitoring workflows to guarantee reliability and rapid incident response.

- Architect repository ecosystems with scalability in mind, leveraging federated and hierarchical topologies as deployment sizes increase.

Through these carefully orchestrated repository management and mirror optimization strategies, large-scale deployments can maintain highly available, performant, and consistent package delivery infrastructures essential for continuous integration, deployment pipelines, and enterprise-grade software distribution.

3.3. Pinning, Masking, and Holding Packages

In complex software ecosystems, managing the versions of installed packages plays a pivotal role in maintaining system stability, security, and compliance with organizational policies. Beyond simple installation and removal, sophisticated version control mechanisms such as package pinning, masking, and holding enable administrators and developers to exercise fine-grained control over package behaviors during upgrades and deployment cycles.

Package *pinning* refers to the explicit specification of a package version or version constraint, thereby preventing automatic upgrades beyond the defined criteria. This technique is indispensable when certain versions of packages have been thoroughly tested and verified within an environment, or when dependencies require strict alignment to ensure compatibility. Pinning is commonly implemented by defining a priority or version preference in configuration files or package manager directives. For example, in systems utilizing the apt package manager, pinning is configured through files in /etc/apt/preferences.d/ using the syntax:

```
Package: <package_name>
Pin: version <version_number>
Pin-Priority: 1001
```

A Pin-Priority value above 1000 forces the package manager to downgrade or prevent upgrades beyond the pinned version, thereby locking the package state. Comprehensive use of pinning supports reproducible system states, particularly in production environments where unanticipated upgrades can introduce regressions or incompatibilities.

Masking packages entails intentionally preventing their installation or upgrade by rendering them unavailable or invisible to the package manager or by assigning them a prohibitive priority. This is typically used to block known vulnerable or deprecated versions from being installed or to comply with compliance policies forbidding certain software. Masking may also involve excluding certain versions from update repositories or overlay feeds. For example, in Gentoo Linux, package masking is implemented by placing package atoms in /etc/portage/package.mask as follows:

```
>=category/package-version
```

Such entries ensure that any attempts to install or upgrade to the masked versions will be blocked, signaling the package manager to report dependency issues rather than proceed with the action. Masking is particularly effective in multi-user or distributed environments where centralized policy enforcement is required to prevent users from unintentionally compromising system integrity.

Package *holding* denotes a persistent state wherein a package is explicitly prevented from being upgraded, often until administrative review or explicit override occurs. Unlike pinning, which can allow some level of controlled upgrading, holding rigidly locks the package at its current version across update cycles. This approach is crucial for critical system components or libraries where upgrades introduce unacceptable risks without comprehensive testing. Package holding can be executed via package manager commands; for example, with dpkg:

```
sudo apt-mark hold <package_name>
```

and can be reversed by:

```
sudo apt-mark unhold <package_name>
```

The distinction between pinning and holding is subtle but important: holding is an explicit action preventing all upgrades, whereas pinning can be more nuanced, allowing selective acceptance of updates matching specific criteria.

The effective combination of pinning, masking, and holding facilitates exemplary control in environments demanding stability and security guarantees. For instance, an enterprise deployment may pin database libraries to validated versions to avoid subtle incompatibilities; simultaneously, mask vulnerable network utilities to comply with security audits; and hold critical kernel modules to ensure hardware compatibility. Selective upgrade policies can then be defined to permit automatic patching of non-critical software, while protecting foundational components.

Implementing these controls demands an understanding of the full dependency graph and awareness of upstream changes, as blocking or freezing package versions without considering dependencies may lead to unresolved conflicts or inconsistent states. Advanced package managers often provide tools to query dependency trees, simulate upgrades, and detect potential conflicts before applying changes.

Security management benefits considerably from masking and holding strategies. Known vulnerable packages can be masked globally to avoid accidental installation, while important security updates for pinned or held packages can be selectively tested and applied. Organizational policies may further mandate the use of these techniques to formally document approved configurations and automate compliance verification.

In multi-repository or multi-branch environments, pinning and masking mechanisms also allow the selective inclusion of software from designated branches, such as stable, testing, or experimental, thereby ensuring that the production environment remains insulated from unstable or unverified releases.

Pinning, masking, and holding form a triad of advanced package management techniques that, when employed discerningly, contribute to system robustness by:

- Maintaining deterministic package versions and minimizing upgrade-induced regressions.

- Enforcing security policies by preventing deployment of vulnerable or unauthorized package versions.

- Supporting compliance with organizational software governance and change control requirements.

- Allowing selective package evolution aligned with organizational risk tolerance and operational priorities.

Mastery of these techniques is critical for administrators and developers operating in large-scale, mission-critical, or security-conscious environments, where the cost of uncontrolled package upgrades can be significant both in downtime and potential system compromise.

3.4. Building and Signing Custom Packages

The process of constructing custom Alpine packages using the abuild system necessitates a disciplined sequence of steps aimed at ensuring reproducibility, integrity, and security. The workflow encompasses securing source code, configuring an isolated build environment, and cryptographically signing the resultant packages for trusted deployment and integration within organizational pipelines.

At the core of abuild is the APKBUILD script, a shell script specifying metadata, source locations, build dependencies, compilation instructions, and packaging directives. Begin by creating an APKBUILD file that precisely declares the package name, version, origin URL, maintainer, license, and dependencies:

```
# Maintainer: Jane Doe <jane.doe@example.com>
pkgname=customlib
pkgver=1.2.3
pkgrel=0
pkgdesc="A custom cryptographic library"
url="https://example.org/customlib"
arch="all"
license="MIT"
depends="libcrypto"
source="https://example.org/customlib/releases/${pkgver
    }/${pkgname}-${pkgver}.tar.gz"
sha512sums="123abc...def456"  # Verify actual hash
```

Securing package sources is fundamental. The source variable should reference immutable origins with cryptographic hash verification performed by abuild during fetching. Establishing sha512sums or appropriate cryptographic checksums guards against tampering. When possible, mirror sources on internal servers that enforce access controls and provenance auditing.

The build environment must be controlled to maintain deterministic outputs. Alpine's abuild facilitates environment isolation through chroot or containerized builds. Prior to building, install abuild and dependencies; then initialize the build environment:

```
# Create build keys and initialize abuild environment
abuild-keygen -a -i
abuild checksum
```

The abuild-keygen command generates cryptographic key pairs used for signing packages and checksums. Private keys must remain protected within secure hardware modules or restricted filesystems. Public keys should be distributed to client systems or CI/CD runners to authenticate package origins.

Building the package inside the prepared environment involves executing:

```
abuild -r
```

The -r flag instructs abuild to perform a full build cycle, including dependency resolution from repositories configured in /etc/apk/repositories. This produces one or more .apk binaries within the packages/ directory.

Cryptographic signing leverages the previously generated keys to ensure authenticity and integrity. By default, abuild signs packages immediately after building, embedding signatures compatible with Alpine's package manager (apk). These signatures enable clients to verify downloaded packages prior to installation, mitigating risks of malicious interference.

Integrating package builds into organizational pipelines requires automation and strict access controls. Continuous integration servers should invoke abuild within ephemeral, fully controlled environments to guarantee reproducibility. Keys used for signing must be managed via hardware security modules (HSMs) or secure vaults, preventing unauthorized use or leakage.

A robust pipeline example abstracts these steps:

- Pull source code tarball and validate checksum.

- Prepare ephemeral build environment with containerization or chroot.

- Run abuild commands to build and generate package.

- Sign package using private keys within secure context.

- Publish .apk to internal repository or artifact storage.

- Notify or trigger downstream deployment systems.

Within repository servers, enforce signature verification by configuring apk-tools to trust only organizational public keys. This establishes a cryptographic chain of trust from build to deployment.

To maintain build environment consistency, control package versions of all build-time dependencies by pinning repositories and mirror snapshots. Utilizing tools such as abuild-deps and apk-convert enables fine-grained control over dependency versions, thereby reducing variability and enhancing security posture.

Finally, maintain thorough audit logs for the entire build and signing lifecycle. Logging key access, build invocation timestamps, and hash comparisons support forensic analysis and compliance requirements. Embedding this rigor within the `abuild` process transforms custom package creation into a resilient, verifiable component of modern DevSecOps workflows.

3.5. Managing System State and Updates

Ensuring safe and reliable system updates necessitates a design approach that rigorously manages system state changes and provides robust mechanisms for recovery in case of failures. The core challenge lies in updating components without disrupting ongoing operations or leaving the system in an inconsistent state. Addressing this challenge involves leveraging design patterns such as transactional upgrades, rollback mechanisms, and snapshot-based recovery, complemented by vigilant monitoring, auditing, and validation processes.

Transactional upgrades operate on the principle that an update to the system should occur atomically—either the entire update succeeds, or the system remains unchanged. This approach draws inspiration from database transaction semantics, extending their guarantees to system software components and configurations. The generalized process involves staging updated components in isolated environments, verifying their integrity and compatibility, and then atomically committing them to the active system. In practice, this often necessitates using transactional file systems or software package managers with transactional capabilities.

For example, adopting a two-phase commit protocol within the update system ensures all components meet preconditions before switching the system state. In the prepare phase, updates are downloaded, verified (e.g., through cryptographic signatures and checksums), and installed into a staging area. Only once all are confirmed valid does the commit phase activate the new components, often via symbolic links or container image swaps, minimizing downtime.

Rollback mechanisms are indispensable complements to transactional updates, providing a safety net when an update introduces regressions or failures undetected during testing. A robust rollback design requires maintaining a precise record of the system's state before and after the update, as well as ensuring the restoration process is itself reliable and fast. Common patterns include versioned backups of configuration files, keeping multiple versions of critical binaries, or leveraging copy-on-write filesystems to revert filesystem states.

Integration of rollback mechanisms often relies on hooks within the update lifecycle. After the commit phase, the system runs validation checks, such as health probes on services, performance assessments, or crash monitors. If any checks fail, automated triggers initiate rollback to the previous known-good state seamlessly. Maintaining metadata around update transactions—timestamps, component versions, checksums—facilitates both manual and automated rollback decisions. To reduce risk, gradual or canary-style rollouts can be combined with rollback policies, restoring only the affected subset if errors arise.

Snapshot-based recovery further enhances system resilience by capturing comprehensive point-in-time images of the system's state. These snapshots encapsulate filesystems, memory state, and application data, enabling restorations that cover scenarios more catastrophic than simple software regression, including configuration corruption or hardware failure. The effectiveness of this pattern depends on efficient snapshot creation, typically requiring support from underlying storage technologies such as copy-on-write or differential block-level snapshots.

Restoration from snapshots can be designed to work in conjunction with transactional upgrades, providing a fall-back when rollback alone is insufficient. For instance, if application state evolves independently of software com-ponents, a rollback might restore executables but leave in-consistent data; snapshots that include data and system state can ensure holistic recovery. The granularity of snap-shots can be tuned depending on system requirements, balancing storage costs against recovery time objectives.

Monitoring and auditing form the operational backbone for ensuring the efficacy and safety of system updates. Real-time monitoring tracks the progress and outcomes of update operations, detecting anomalies such as prolonged update durations, partial failures, or unexpected system behavior after deployment. Integrating lightweight health checks, resource utilization monitors, and application-specific verification scripts allows for rapid detection of issues.

Auditing, by contrast, is concerned with the comprehen-sive logging and retention of update-related activities for post-mortem analysis and compliance. Audit logs typ-ically record the identity of the initiating entity, times-tamps, pre-update and post-update states, validation out-comes, and rollback events. Secure and tamper-evident audit trails are critical in regulated or mission-critical environments to provide traceability and accountability.

Validation mechanisms complement monitoring by providing systematic checks that ensure the consistency, correctness, and performance of the system after updates. This may involve automated testing frameworks that run integration or regression tests immediately following an update, as well as formal verification techniques for critical components. Validation scripts integrated into the update workflow can block promotion of updates if tests fail, thus acting as gatekeepers prior to live deployment.

Together, these design patterns and operational practices create a comprehensive framework for managing system state and updates with high reliability. The use of transactional upgrades, rollback mechanisms, and snapshot-based recovery ensures that system changes are atomic, reversible, and restorable, while monitoring, auditing, and validation provide continuous assurance and visibility. Implementations must carefully tailor these patterns to the specific system architecture, operational constraints, and risk tolerance, always aiming to minimize disruption and preserve system integrity throughout the update lifecycle.

3.6. Security, Integrity, and Compliance

Ensuring the provenance, authenticity, and regulatory compliance of software deployed on Alpine Linux mandates a multilayered approach that integrates cryptographic verification, robust policy enforcement, and comprehensive compliance auditing. Alpine Linux, valued for its minimalism and security-oriented design, inherently supports mechanisms critical for maintaining a trustworthy software ecosystem. This section delineates best practices centered on these three pillars, tailored to regulated environments demanding stringent controls over software supply chains.

Cryptographic Integrity Checks

Alpine Linux employs a variety of cryptographic tools to uphold the integrity and authenticity of software packages. Packages distributed through Alpine's apk package manager include embedded cryptographic signatures, primarily utilizing OpenPGP-based mechanisms. This design enables clients to verify both the integrity (ensuring no tampering) and provenance (confirming origin) of packages before installation.

The cornerstone of package verification within Alpine is the trust model established by apk-tools, which checks signatures against locally stored public keys. To enforce this:

- Maintain a strict and auditable keyring of trusted maintainers' public keys, housed under secure access controls and updated via authenticated channels.

- Regularly rotate keys and revoke compromised or deprecated ones using standard OpenPGP key management protocols.

- Leverage checksum verification using SHA-256 or stronger algorithms, matching package manifests to their signed hashes.

Control files like APKINDEX.tar.gz are signed to provide an immutable ledger of the package metadata. Automated scripts should be deployed to verify these signatures pre-installation, rejecting any unsigned or improperly signed packages.

Integrating hardware security modules (HSMs) or secure enclaves for key storage and signing operations further enhances authenticity guarantees, minimizing exposure to key compromise. Furthermore, implementation of reproducible builds contributes to verifiable provenance, permitting downstream users to reconstruct binaries from source and match cryptographic hashes.

Policy Enforcement Mechanisms

For regulated environments, deploying software devoid of contextual policy controls introduces compliance risks. Alpine Linux installations must incorporate policy engines and mandatory access controls (MAC) to restrict software execution based on defined parameters.

- Utilize Linux Security Modules (LSMs) such as AppArmor, SELinux, or Tomoyo to enforce execution policies at the kernel level. These frameworks govern how binaries interact with system resources, drastically reducing attack surfaces.

- Apply Software Bill of Materials (SBOM) policies specifying allowed software inventory, versions, and patch levels. apk tooling can be extended with scripts or hooks to audit installed packages against approved lists prior to deployment.

- Enforce runtime integrity checks via tools like AIDE (Advanced Intrusion Detection Environment) or Tripwire, which monitor critical filesystem objects by verifying cryptographic hashes and alerting on alterations.

- Integrate runtime application self-protection (RASP) or endpoint detection and response (EDR) solutions compatible with Alpine environments to continuously monitor behavioral integrity.

75

Policies should be codified using automated configuration management and infrastructure-as-code (IaC) frameworks, ensuring reproducibility and auditability. Tools such as Open Policy Agent (OPA) can be deployed to encode complex policy rules governing package acceptance, deployment, and execution within orchestrated Alpine-based clusters.

Compliance Audit Tools for Regulated Environments

Meeting regulatory mandates-such as GDPR, HIPAA, PCI-DSS, or industry-specific frameworks-requires comprehensive audit trails and demonstrable compliance at every stage of software lifecycle management.

Alpine Linux's lightweight architecture accommodates the inclusion of compliance-specific tooling without significant resource overhead:

- Use OpenSCAP to perform automated compliance scanning against predefined security baselines and regulatory standards. Custom Alpine profiles can be generated aligning with organizational policies.

- Implement logging and centralized audit frameworks (e.g., syslog-ng or rsyslog forwarding to SIEM systems) configured to capture package installation events, signature verification results, and policy enforcement actions with timestamps and user context.

- Employ immutable ledger technologies such as blockchain-based provenance registries to record cryptographically signed software deployment transactions, enabling tamper-evident audit trails.

- Integrate continuous compliance monitoring within

CI/CD pipelines using tools tailored for Alpine containers, ensuring every software update complies with regulatory policies before reaching production.

Extracting detailed SBOMs from Alpine environments enhances visibility for auditors. Tools like syft can generate comprehensive manifests inclusive of package metadata, licenses, and cryptographic hashes, enabling downstream compliance analysis.

Synthesis of Practices

A robust security posture on Alpine Linux platforms hinges upon automating cryptographic verifications at install time, enforcing granular software execution policies, and maintaining immutable audit records for compliance evidence. By fusing cryptographic integrity with policy enforcement and compliance tooling, organizations can create a verifiable chain of trust from source code to runtime environment.

The continuous integration of these controls into deployment pipelines, coupled with secure key management and reproducible build practices, minimizes risks of software supply chain attacks-a critical concern in contemporary cybersecurity. Embracing these best practices delivers assurance not only to system administrators but also to auditors and regulatory bodies, ultimately safeguarding operational integrity within highly regulated ecosystems.

Chapter 4

System Configuration and Core Services

Every reliable system stands on a foundation of thoughtful configuration and resilient core services. In this chapter, you'll discover the art and science behind Alpine Linux's configuration philosophy—from managing essential system files to orchestrating services at scale. Explore practical strategies to streamline administration, enforce policy, and empower users—ensuring your Alpine deployments remain robust, manageable, and secure whether running on a single server or across thousands.

4.1. OpenRC and Init System Deep Dive

Alpine Linux's selection of OpenRC as its init system reflects a strategic preference for simplicity, speed, and modularity, setting it apart from more complex alternatives such as systemd. OpenRC is designed to be a dependency-based init system that avoids reliance on PID files, enhancing reliability and predictability across diverse usage scenarios. Its design philosophy emphasizes straightforward yet powerful mechanisms for service management, customizable through advanced features such as custom runlevels, explicit dependency declarations, and fine-grained control of startup sequencing.

OpenRC's architecture revolves around init scripts typically located in /etc/init.d/, with service states managed through symbolic links under runlevel directories, analogous to the System V init style but augmented with dependency resolution. The concept of runlevels in OpenRC is extended through customizable directories representing service groups tailored for specific system states or modes, such as multi-user, graphical, or rescue environments.

Custom Runlevels and Service Groups

Custom runlevels serve as an effective tool to tailor service activation sets diverse to operational contexts. For example, one might define a runlevel networking-critical dedicated only to minimal networking essentials, or container-runtime for container host service activation. Creating and managing a custom runlevel involves establishing a runlevel directory under /etc/runlevels/ and populating it with symbolic links to the required service scripts.

```
mkdir /etc/runlevels/container-runtime
```

```
rc-update add docker container-runtime
ln -s /etc/init.d/docker /etc/runlevels/container-
    runtime/docker
```

This capability facilitates strict control over which services are active, optimizing resource usage and security posture by minimizing unnecessary service activation.

Service Dependencies and Fine-Grained Control

OpenRC's dependency mechanism is declared within each service script via keywords such as depend(), enabling explicit control over the activation order. Dependencies can be marked as need, use, or before/after, influencing both hard and soft requirements to ensure robust startup sequences.

Consider a service webapp that requires the networking and database services. Its init script should declare these dependencies as follows:

```
depend() {
    need networking database
    after firewall
    use logger
}
```

Here, need enforces the presence of networking and database before webapp starts; after ensures firewall initializes earlier without enforcing a strict requirement; use is a soft dependency allowing webapp to start regardless of logger presence but leveraging it if available.

This flexible dependency specification allows crafting deterministic startup orders while gracefully handling optional services to improve resilience.

Orchestrating Startup Order

OpenRC automatically resolves dependencies to orchestrate a coherent initialization sequence. However, advanced control over specific service start timing can be encoded via explicit ordering directives within the depend() function.

For systems requiring complex orchestration, such as multi-stage services or those with conditional initialization phases (e.g., database migration followed by API startup), one can implement:

```
depend() {
    need localmount
    before webapp
}

start_pre() {
    /usr/local/bin/db-migrate.sh
}
```

In this model, localmount is guaranteed before the service begins, and the start_pre hook allows pre-start operations such as schema migrations to complete, minimizing race conditions. Furthermore, leveraging before ensures the service initiates prior to webapp, orchestrating interdependent services carefully.

Building Reliable and Recoverable Service Infrastructures

Reliability and recoverability in the OpenRC ecosystem hinge on exploiting its inherent features combined with disciplined scripting. Implementing exit-status-based watchdog patterns within service scripts and incorporating retry logic in start() functions helps to maintain service continuity.

A typical recovery strategy incorporates check and restart actions leveraging OpenRC's monitoring commands:

```
start() {
    ebegin "Starting myservice"
```

```
    start-stop-daemon --start --quiet --exec /usr/local/
    bin/myservice
    eend $?
}

stop() {
    ebegin "Stopping myservice"
    start-stop-daemon --stop --quiet --exec /usr/local/
    bin/myservice
    eend $?
}

restart() {
    stop
    start
}

check() {
    if ! pgrep myservice > /dev/null; then
        eerror "myservice not running, restarting..."
        restart
    else
        ebegin "myservice running"
        eend 0
    fi
}
```

Service supervisors or cron jobs can execute the `check` action at intervals, ensuring automatic service healing. OpenRC further supports integration with monitoring tools via standardized status queries `rc-service <service> status`, facilitating centralized orchestration.

Alpine's embrace of OpenRC mitigates the complexity seen in monolithic init systems while providing ample flexibility to engineer dependable service infrastructures. Custom runlevels allow minimalist and scenario-specific environments, explicit dependency management guarantees sound startup order, and scripting hooks enable building robust health checks and orchestrations. Mastery of these advanced capabilities ensures architects can construct Alpine-based systems that are both performant and resilient, meeting stringent availability and maintainability demands.

4.2. System Configuration Files and Policies

Alpine Linux, renowned for its minimalism and security-oriented design, relies fundamentally on a straightforward yet powerful hierarchy of configuration files and policy overlays that dictate system behavior. Understanding these key components is critical for effective system administration, especially in environments requiring centralized policy enforcement, templating, and consistent configuration management across heterogeneous deployments.

At the core of Alpine's system configuration lies the /etc directory, a conventional locus for global configuration files. Unlike some distributions that obfuscate system settings behind abstractions, Alpine maintains readability and simplicity by providing clear, mostly plain-text files that can be directly edited or templated. A particularly important file is /etc/network/interfaces, where network interfaces are declared using a Debian-derived syntax. This file governs interface initialization, IP addressing, and routing, thus enabling predictable network setup on boot.

Another pivotal configuration file is /etc/apk/repositories. Alpine Package Keeper (APK), the native package manager, references this file to locate repositories and mirrors from which packages and updates are retrieved. Administrators can manipulate this file to point systems to custom or local mirrors, enabling faster, secure, and policy-compliant software provisioning across a fleet. This is essential for centralized control over software sources as well as minimizing untrusted external dependencies.

84

System-wide security policies and service configurations are also primarily influenced by /etc/rc.conf. This file adopts a simple key-value format and controls service enablement flags, runtime options, and logging verbosity. For example, toggling sshd=YES enables the SSH daemon at boot, thereby standardizing service availability. The clarity of this file facilitates automated templating and version control, where changes can be scripted or deployed via configuration management tools without parsing complications.

Overlay technology in Alpine manifests prominently via /etc/apkovl.tar.gz, a compressed archive file that serves as the system overlay mechanism during early boot. This overlay includes custom user configurations, SSH keys, scripts, and other local customizations that extend or override the base Alpine system image. It functions analogously to a union filesystem overlay, allowing immutable base system architectures to be augmented securely without altering the underlying image. Administrators create and manage overlays using the alpine-mkuimage and libalpine-virt tools, embedding consistent configuration across multiple installations while preserving system immutability.

For more granular or complex policy enforcement, Alpine harnesses the extensibility of the OpenRC init system. Extended service definitions, dependency chains, and boot-time constraints are encoded in /etc/init.d/ scripts and enhanced with policy files located in /etc/conf.d/. The concept of service profiles here enables precise control over system state; for instance, administrators can define specific environment variables in conf.d files to tailor runtime behavior for services uniformly across multiple hosts.

Centralized policy enforcement extends naturally into

Alpine's integration with configuration management frameworks such as Ansible, Puppet, or SaltStack. Alpine's simple configuration files are particularly amenable to templating using Jinja2 or similar engines. Templates abstract repetitive configuration patterns by populating variables and conditionals externally, resulting in consistent, reproducible system states. Maintaining configuration in version-controlled repositories ensures traceability and auditability of changes while supporting rollback capabilities.

A common technique for enforcing consistent system policies involves creating a unified repository of configuration templates and policy overlays stored in a version control system. Through automated deployment pipelines, these templates can be rendered and applied to target systems dynamically, ensuring configuration drift is minimized. Integrating Alpine's package repositories and overlay archives into this pipeline allows simultaneous management of software updates and configuration policies.

Moreover, Alpine's lightweight nature enables it to be deployed in containers and virtualized environments where configuration consistency is paramount. Utilizing the overlay concept combined with templated /etc files, identical policy and service states can be projected onto ephemeral instances, facilitating rapid scaling without configuration discrepancies.

To illustrate practical application, consider templating the network interface configuration /etc/network/interfaces for a dynamically provisioned Alpine host. A Jinja2 template might be structured as follows:

```
auto eth0
iface eth0 inet static
   address {{ ip_address }}
```

```
netmask {{ netmask }}
gateway {{ gateway }}
dns-nameservers {{ dns_servers | join(' ') }}
```

Populating this template with host-specific variables prior to deployment ensures uniform syntax with tailored network parameters.

Similarly, centralized management of the APK repositories file can guarantee usage of approved mirrors:

```
{{ repository_mirror }}
{{ testing_repo }}
{{ community_repo }}
```

Application of such templated overlays facilitates automatic rollback by regenerating /etc/apkovl.tar.gz images, reducing administrative overhead.

Alpine's system configuration files and overlay mechanisms provide a powerful, modular approach to governing system behavior. Their design simplicity, combined with the power of templating and policy overlays, equips administrators to maintain rigorous control over complex, distributed Alpine environments. Mastery of these configuration control techniques is indispensable for scalable, secure, and compliant Alpine Linux operations.

4.3. User, Group, and Privilege Leadership

Modern system administration demands refined control over user identities, group memberships, and their associated privileges to enforce secure and efficient access management. Moving beyond basic user account creation and group classification, advanced frameworks leverage granular privilege assignment, sophisticated sudo configurations, and Pluggable Authentication Module (PAM) integration to accommodate complex security policies without compromising usability.

At the core of privilege leadership is the principle of least privilege, which prescribes that users and processes be granted only the minimal rights necessary to perform their tasks. Implementing this principle requires decomposing system capabilities into fine-grained permissions, typically managed through a combination of user accounts, groups, and access control lists. Group membership serves as a primary vector for collective privilege enforcement, enabling administrators to define roles that aggregate relevant permissions. However, overly broad group assignments risk privilege escalation, which mandates careful delineation and frequent audits.

Privilege delegation is elegantly facilitated by sudo, a tool that enables permitted users to execute specific commands with elevated privileges. Beyond simple all-or-nothing elevation, sudo supports granular configuration through its /etc/sudoers file, where administrators specify user-command mappings, host restrictions, and custom environment parameters. This mechanism allows compartmentalizing administrative functions, such as permitting a user to restart network services without granting full root access.

A sample sudoers configuration excerpt exemplifies this granularity:

```
# Allow 'netadmin' group to restart network services
%netadmin ALL=(root) NOPASSWD: /bin/systemctl restart
    network.service

# Permit user 'alice' to edit configuration files with
    vim
alice ALL=(root) /usr/bin/vim /etc/nginx/nginx.conf
```

88

In the above, the `netadmin` group is enabled to restart the network service via `systemctl` without re-entering passwords, streamlining operational workflow while maintaining auditability. User `alice` is constrained strictly to editing the specified configuration file, avoiding broader root shell access.

To further refine authentication processes, administrators integrate **Pluggable Authentication Modules (PAM)**. PAM provides a modular framework allowing customization of authentication, authorization, and session management policies independently from applications. This modularity supports enforcing multi-factor authentication, restricting logins based on time or network location, and incorporating centralized identity services. By adjusting PAM configuration files, typically found under `/etc/pam.d/`, systems can demand complex authentication schemes tailored to organizational security postures.

An example PAM rule sequence for SSH authentication might be:

```
auth required pam_google_authenticator.so
auth required pam_unix.so try_first_pass
account required pam_time.so
```

Here, authentication requires a valid Google Authenticator token, followed by standard password verification, and accounts are subject to temporal login restrictions. Through such stacks, PAM permits layered enforcement without modifying individual service code.

Balancing usability against strict least-privilege requirements often entails trade-offs. Highly restrictive policies can impair user productivity and lead to risky workarounds, such as users sharing privileged accounts or disabling security features. To mitigate this, privilege leadership must emphasize role-based access control (RBAC), where roles encapsulate sets of permissions reflecting organizational units and job functions. Dynamic group membership tools, including directory services like LDAP or Active Directory, can synchronize roles with user lifecycle events, minimizing manual overhead.

Additionally, secure delegation frameworks such as sudo time-limit options, command logging, and user notifications elevate accountability. Coupling these with PAM's ability to enforce contextual constraints-such as requiring additional authentication for sensitive commands-offers layered defense in depth.

Effective privilege management benefits from ongoing monitoring and periodic privilege reviews. Use of audit tools and system logs can detect anomalies, such as unexpected sudo usage patterns or login attempts violating PAM policies. Automated analyses can flag orphaned accounts, excessive group memberships, and unused privilege grants, enabling timely pruning to uphold minimal exposure.

Advanced user, group, and privilege leadership employs a combination of granular sudo configurations, flexible PAM authentication strategies, and dynamic group-role mappings to enforce the principle of least privilege while preserving operational efficiency. This multifaceted approach addresses the evolving landscape of system security by integrating policy enforcement, auditability, and user-centric design to create resilient and manageable access control ecosystems.

4.4. Locale, Timezone, and Time Synchronization

System-level configuration of locale and timezone settings serves as a foundational step in internationalization, enabling software to appropriately adapt user interfaces, data formats, and time representations according to regional preferences. The locale encapsulates language, country, and variant preferences used for sorting, formatting numbers, dates, currencies, and textual messages, while the timezone dictates the local time offset relative to Coordinated Universal Time (UTC).

Setting the locale on modern Unix-like systems typically involves defining environment variables such as LANG and LC_* variables. A canonical example is:

```
export LANG=en_US.UTF-8
export LC_TIME=fr_FR.UTF-8
```

Here, LANG sets the default locale globally, while LC_TIME overrides the time and date formatting to French conventions. The suffix UTF-8 specifies the character encoding. The locale definitions reside under /usr/share/i18n/locales and /usr/lib/locale, and must be generated and installed via utilities like locale-gen on Debian-based systems.

Timezone configuration centers on selecting the appropriate zoneinfo database entry, which is maintained under /usr/share/zoneinfo. The system's current timezone is most commonly designated by the symbolic link at /etc/localtime pointing to a specific timezone file, for example, America/New_York. The command-line utility timedatectl provides a streamlined interface for status querying and modification:

```
timedatectl set-timezone Europe/Paris
```

91

```
timedatectl status
```

Automating internationalization across distributed systems, especially in cloud and containerized deployments, requires explicit locale and timezone provisioning in environment variables or container runtime parameters. Immutable container images often embed locale and timezone data explicitly, accommodating runtime overrides. For example, in Docker, environment variables can be supplied during container instantiation:

```
docker run -e LANG=de_DE.UTF-8 -e TZ=Europe/Berlin myapp
```

Furthermore, programmatic internationalization interfaces, such as the ICU (International Components for Unicode) library, depend on correctly set locales to provide localized formats.

The integrity of temporal data across distributed architectures hinges on accurate and synchronized clocks. Time synchronization mechanisms are vital, as discrepancies can impair logging, distributed databases, time-based access controls, and cryptographic protocols. The Network Time Protocol (NTP) remains a pervasive solution, leveraging hierarchical servers to disseminate reliable time references. However, its classical implementations can suffer from drift, network asymmetry, and stratum inaccuracies.

More recent and precise alternatives include the Precision Time Protocol (PTP), standardized as IEEE 1588, which achieves submicrosecond accuracy primarily in localized network environments, and Chrony, a versatile NTP client and server optimized for systems with intermittent network connectivity or virtualized platforms.

High-precision time synchronization leverages hardware timestamping capabilities and disciplined clocks, such as GPS receivers or atomic clocks integrated with local Network Time Servers (NTS). NTS extends NTP with crypto-graphic security and session-based exchanges, enhancing trustworthiness in public networks.

Clock drift-a gradual divergence of the system clock from the reference time-is a recurrent issue due to hardware os-cillator imperfections and environmental factors like tem-perature variability. Continuous monitoring of system clock offset and frequency is necessary; this is routinely performed by time synchronization daemons via phase-locked loops and frequency correction.

Diagnostics for drift involve tools such as ntpq (for NTP), chronyc (for Chrony), or timedatectl. For example, chronyc tracking reports offset, frequency, and stability metrics:

```
Reference ID    : 123.45.67.89 (time-source.example.com)
Stratum         : 3
Ref time (UTC)  : Thu Apr 25 12:34:56 2024
System time     : 0.000003 seconds slow of NTP time
Frequency       : 15.123 ppm slow
Residual freq   : +0.234 ppm
Skew            : 1.234 ppm
Root delay      : 0.01234 seconds
Root dispersion: 0.00123 seconds
```

Persistent drift or large offsets may indicate configuration errors, network latency asymmetry, or failing hardware clocks, warranting further examination or redundancy ad-dition with multiple time sources.

In distributed environments, consistent timekeeping also necessitates awareness of leap seconds and daylight saving time (DST) adjustments. Systems typically process time internally as UTC, converting to local times only at the user interface layer. Approaches avoid local timezone depen-dence in timestamps (favoring ISO 8601 or UNIX epoch time) to ensure uniformity and ease correlation across nodes in event logs or transaction records.

Ensuring robust time synchronization and locale correctness demands a layered strategy:

- Explicitly define locale and timezone settings system-wide and per application scope.

- Employ automated configuration management for consistent deployment in heterogeneous environments.

- Utilize high-precision synchronization protocols matched to network topology and precision requirements.

- Monitor drift continuously and incorporate redundancy in upstream time sources.

- Design applications to internalize time representation in UTC, applying locale-aware transformations only at output boundaries.

Through these mechanisms, software systems achieve resilient internationalization and accurate temporal coherence, essential for globalized digital infrastructure and real-time data integrity.

4.5. Monitoring and Logging Architectures

Effective monitoring and logging architectures form the backbone of robust system observability, compliance, and incident response strategies in modern IT environments. This section expounds on configuring syslog, managing rotating logs, employing auditing frameworks, and establishing remote log aggregation, thereby providing comprehensive guidance for maintaining system integrity and operational visibility.

Syslog is the de facto standard for forwarding log messages in UNIX-like systems, enabling centralized log collection and processing. Configuration of syslog involves specifying the sources, message formats, and destinations. Common syslog daemons such as rsyslog or syslog-ng provide flexible configuration syntaxes to filter, transform, and route log data.

A basic rsyslog configuration to collect local kernel and application logs and forward them to a remote host at IP 192.168.1.100 on UDP port 514 may be constructed as follows:

```
# Load necessary modules
module(load="imuxsock")    # local system logging
module(load="imklog")      # kernel logging

# Define global directives
global(workDirectory="/var/spool/rsyslog")

# Send all messages to remote log server
*.* @192.168.1.100:514
```

The single asterisk wildcard *.* captures all facilities and priorities, ensuring comprehensive log forwarding. For improved reliability, TCP can replace UDP by using @@ instead of @ in the destination line to guarantee delivery through connection-oriented transport.

Continuous logging risks saturating disk resources, rendering systems unstable or causing data loss. Log rotation policies mitigate these risks by archiving and optionally compressing logs regularly, while purging old entries.

The GNU logrotate utility automates rotation, with configurations specifying rotation frequency, compression, retention, and scripting hooks. A typical logrotate configuration snippet targeting /var/log/syslog might be:

95

```
/var/log/syslog {
    daily
    rotate 7
    compress
    delaycompress
    missingok
    notifempty
    create 0640 root adm
    postrotate
        systemctl reload rsyslog.service > /dev/null
    2>&1 || true
    endscript
}
```

Here, logs rotate daily, retaining seven archives, compressing all but the most recent rotated file. The postrotate script reloads rsyslog, ensuring that newly created logs are handled correctly. Proper permissions ensure only authorized users access sensitive logs.

Beyond generic logging, auditing frameworks provide granular, tamper-resistant tracking of system events critical for compliance and forensic analysis. The Linux Audit System (auditd) is a widely adopted solution conforming to the Common Criteria and various regulatory requirements.

Rules within auditd define which events are recorded. For example, to audit write attempts to the /etc/passwd file:

```
auditctl -w /etc/passwd -p wa -k passwd_changes
```

This rule watches the /etc/passwd file for writes and attribute changes, tagging log entries with the key passwd_changes. Audit logs captured in /var/log/audit/audit.log are immutable unless root privileges modify or delete the files, and centralized logging of audit data strengthens tamper evidence.

Consolidating logs from multiple systems enhances monitoring efficiency, incident detection, and historical analysis. Solutions such as the Elastic Stack (formerly ELK: Elasticsearch, Logstash, Kibana) or Graylog ingest logs centrally, providing indexing, search, visualization, and alerting functionalities.

A common architectural approach involves deploying lightweight log shippers like `Filebeat` or `Fluentd` on endpoints to forward logs to a centralized processing node running `Logstash`. After ingest, logs are indexed in Elasticsearch and accessed through Kibana dashboards.

Key considerations when deploying remote aggregation include:

- **Secure transport:** TLS-encrypted channels and authentication mechanisms (e.g., mutual TLS or API tokens) prevent interception and unauthorized submission.

- **Scalability:** High-throughput log pipelines require load balancing, buffering, and redundancy to maintain availability under peak loads.

- **Data normalization:** Parsers and grok patterns in Logstash transform heterogeneous log formats into structured JSON documents for efficient querying.

- **Retention policies:** Indexed data is retained based on compliance or operational needs, with automated rolled indices and archival procedures.

An example `Filebeat` configuration excerpt to send system logs securely to a Logstash server:

```
filebeat.inputs:
- type: log
  enabled: true
  paths:
    - /var/log/syslog
    - /var/log/auth.log
```

```
output.logstash:
  hosts: ["logstash.example.com:5044"]
  ssl.enabled: true
  ssl.certificate_authorities: ["/etc/pki/tls/certs/
    logstash-ca.pem"]
```

Incorporating monitoring and logging architectures within incident response workflows requires fine-grained log collection, real-time alerts, and forensic readiness. Essential practices include:

- Ensuring logs contain sufficient contextual information such as timestamps with nanosecond precision, process identifiers, and correlation IDs.

- Implementing anomaly detection and threshold-based alerting mechanisms integrated with Security Information and Event Management (SIEM) solutions.

- Maintaining an audit trail that can be cryptographically verified for authenticity, supporting incident investigation and regulatory audits.

- Periodic validation of logging configurations and rotation policies to prevent data loss during failovers or system upgrades.

Ultimately, a layered logging architecture that combines system-level logs, audit frameworks, and centralized aggregation enhances observability, enforces compliance mandates, and equips administrators to swiftly detect and mitigate incidents.

4.6. Backup Strategies and System Snapshots

A resilient backup strategy is imperative for maintaining system integrity and ensuring swift recovery in the event of hardware failure, data corruption, or cyber threats. Alpine Linux, known for its minimalistic and security-oriented design, requires tailored backup methodologies that leverage lightweight and efficient tools while maintaining robustness. Core to these methodologies are incremental and differential backup techniques, system snapshots, and automated recovery plans that can handle both single-device restorations and large-scale fleet management.

Incremental and differential backups each optimize storage efficiency and recovery speed but differ fundamentally in approach. Incremental backups save only the data changed since the last backup of any type (full or incremental), resulting in smaller, more frequent backup sets. In contrast, differential backups save data changed since the last full backup, aggregating all changes and enabling quicker recovery at the expense of increasing backup sizes over time.

Alpine environments benefit from tools like `rsync` and `tar` combined with snapshotting filesystems or layered backup utilities such as `BorgBackup` or `Restic`, which support deduplication and encryption. A typical incremental backup setup using `rsync` over SSH can be scripted as follows:

```
#!/bin/sh
SOURCE="/etc /home /var"
DEST="/mnt/backup/alpine"
DATE=$(date +%Y-%m-%d)
LINK_DEST="$DEST/latest"

rsync -a --delete --link-dest=$LINK_DEST $SOURCE $DEST/
    $DATE
```

```
rm -f $DEST/latest
ln -s $DEST/$DATE $DEST/latest
```

Here, the --link-dest option creates hard links to unchanged files from the previous snapshot, preserving file
system metadata and minimizing storage consumption.
This combination effectively creates incremental backups
while maintaining the appearance of full snapshots for
ease of recovery.

Differential backups, while less common in Unix-like
systems where filesystem snapshots prevail, can be
implemented by capturing changed files since the last
full backup using change detection through find or
checksum databases. However, their use in Alpine is
often subsumed by snapshot-based methodologies.

Alpine supports several copy-on-write (CoW) filesystems,
including btrfs and overlayfs. These filesystems enable
instantaneous snapshots with minimal storage overhead,
capturing the exact state of the filesystem at a point in
time.

btrfs is particularly advantageous because it integrates
built-in snapshot management, incremental send/receive
for efficient backup replication, and data integrity verification. A snapshot can be created non-disruptively using:

```
btrfs subvolume snapshot /mnt/data /mnt/data_snap_$(date
    +%Y%m%d)
```

Automated snapshot rotation can be scripted incorporating pruning policies to limit disk usage by removing snapshots older than a threshold. For disaster recovery, btrfs
send and receive commands facilitate incremental transfer of snapshots to remote or detached storage:

```
btrfs send -p /mnt/data_snap_20240401 /mnt/
    data_snap_20240407 | ssh backup@remote-server btrfs
    receive /backup/volume
```

100

Overlay filesystems, such as `overlayfs`, are typically used in containerized environments found in Alpine deployments. While they do not natively support snapshots at the filesystem level, snapshot-like behavior can be emulated through layered image management tools such as `Docker` or `podman`, with image tagging serving as version points.

Backup systems are only as effective as their ability to restore reliably and promptly. Automated restore plans ensure minimal downtime and human error during recovery. A best practice involves maintaining scripted procedures for:

- Verification of backup integrity prior to restoration using checksums or tool-specific verification commands (`borg check`, `restic check`).

- Restoration of files or entire system images with automated verification post-restoration for completeness.

- Sequential recovery in case of incremental backup chains, restoring the last full backup followed by each incremental in order.

An example restoration command for a backup made with `rsync` with snapshot hard links may be as simple as switching symbolic links to the desired snapshot:

```
rm -rf /mnt/restore
cp -al /mnt/backup/alpine/2024-04-07 /mnt/restore
```

For more complex images, system recovery could involve booting from a rescue image and restoring file system snapshots or full disk images using `dd`, `partclone`, or `btrfs` tools.

System imaging complements file-level backups by capturing the entire system state, including bootloader, partitions, and configurations. This is critical in scenarios involving catastrophic failures or mass redeployment of Alpine systems in fleet environments.

Primary tools for disk imaging include `Clonezilla`, `partclone`, and `fsarchiver`, capable of producing compressed filesystem snapshots and bare-metal restore media. For immutable Alpine images, creating a read-only system image using squashfs or overlayfs decreases recovery time and simplifies fleet consistency management.

In automated fleet management, image deployment can be orchestrated through PXE boot environments combined with NFS or HTTP servers hosting the base images alongside configuration management tools like `Ansible`, `Salt`, or `Terraform`. Integrating incremental snapshot transfers with system imaging frameworks provides a balance of efficient updates and system consistency.

A representative workflow involves:

- Periodic creation of full system images and storage on a central server.

- Application of incremental `btrfs` snapshots or `rsync` delta backups for update cycles.

- Remote deployment or restoration via PXE boot and scripted provisioning.

Such an approach ensures rapid, scalable recovery from failures or migration to new hardware within Alpine fleets, with minimal network bandwidth usage and centralized management.

Combining incremental and differential backups with filesystem snapshotting and full system imaging creates a versatile and efficient backup environment tailored for Alpine. Automation through scripting and integration with standard Linux tools, supplemented by Alpine's modularity, ensures that backup and recovery protocols remain both lightweight and robust. Clear restore plans and fleet-oriented imaging methodologies further heighten resilience, minimize downtime, and optimize resource use across diverse deployment scenarios.

Chapter 5

Networking: Configuration and Security

Networking is the nervous system of modern infrastructure—and with Alpine Linux, you have the nimbleness to craft anything from streamlined private networks to robust, security-hardened production topologies. This chapter takes you deep into the configuration, optimization, and protection of Alpine's networking stack, revealing proven techniques and clever strategies to build, scale, and defend any network—no matter the complexity or threat landscape.

5.1. Network Interface Provisioning

Network interface provisioning is a critical aspect of system configuration, dictating how a host communicates within a network. It involves specifying IP addressing schemes, interface names, and advanced interface parameters to ensure optimal performance and consistent behavior. This section elaborates on provisioning methodologies centered around udev and netifrc, explains static versus dynamic IP addressing, emphasizes the importance of predictable interface naming, and explores techniques for performance tuning. Additionally, troubleshooting guidance and automation strategies are discussed to facilitate rapid and reliable deployment.

Interface Naming via udev

Predictable and stable interface naming is a foundation for manageable network configuration. The udev subsystem in Linux provides dynamic device management and is instrumental in assigning persistent names to network interfaces based on hardware attributes such as MAC addresses, PCI bus location, or interface types.

Configuration involves creating custom udev rules, typically placed in /etc/udev/rules.d/. A canonical example of a rule to assign a fixed name to a network interface by MAC address is:

```
SUBSYSTEM=="net", ACTION=="add", ATTR{address
    }=="00:11:22:33:44:55", NAME="eth0"
```

Here, every time a device with the matching MAC address is detected, it receives the name eth0. This avoids issues from interface renaming on reboot or hardware changes. For more flexible naming, udev supports more complex matching expressions using device attributes or parent devices.

Configuring Interfaces with netifrc

netifrc is a framework primarily used in Gentoo and similar distributions for network interface configuration, providing a consistent interface for both static and dynamic setups. Interfaces are configured via scripts typically located in /etc/conf.d/net, with service management through OpenRC or similar init systems.

Static IP Configuration

Static IP configuration in netifrc requires setting explicit values for address, netmask, gateway, and DNS servers. An example configuration snippet for the eth0 interface could be:

```
config_eth0="192.168.1.100/24"
routes_eth0="default via 192.168.1.1"
dns_servers_eth0="8.8.8.8 8.8.4.4"
```

This explicitly states the static IP, netmask (via CIDR), default route, and DNS resolvers. The netifrc scripts use this data to bring interfaces up on boot or during a network service restart.

Dynamic IP Configuration using DHCP

To enable dynamic IP address acquisition via DHCP, netifrc uses the DHCP client integrated into the system (often dhcpcd or dhclient). The interface configuration for eth0 is simplified:

```
config_eth0="dhcp"
```

This instructs the interface to obtain IP addressing, routing, and DNS configuration automatically at runtime. Additional DHCP options such as hostname broadcast or client identifier can be appended via hooks or DHCP client configuration files.

Advanced Interface Tuning

Beyond basic addressing and naming, network interfaces benefit from performance tuning to meet specific workload demands. Such tuning often applies to parameters exposed via ethtool, ip, or sysfs:

- **Offloading Features:** Enabling or disabling features like TCP segmentation offload (TSO), generic segmentation offload (GSO), or checksum offloading can significantly affect throughput and CPU usage.

- **Interrupt Moderation:** Adjusting interrupt coalescing parameters reduces CPU interrupt load at high traffic, configurable via ethtool.

- **MTU Settings:** Modifying the Maximum Transmission Unit (MTU) allows for larger frames (e.g., Jumbo Frames) to reduce overhead on high-speed LANs.

- **Queue Configuration:** Tuning the number of transmit and receive queues or enabling multi-queue allows better parallelism on multicore systems.

A typical command to tune interrupt moderation on eth0 is shown below:

```
ethtool -C eth0 rx-usecs 50 tx-usecs 50
```

Troubleshooting Network Interface Setup

Network provisioning often encounters issues related to interface recognition, incorrect addressing, or misapplied settings. Systematic troubleshooting improves reliability:

- **Check Interface State:** Use ip link show to confirm interface presence and state.

- **Validate Addresses and Routes:** Commands ip addr show and ip route verify assigned IPs and routing tables.

- **Service Status:** When using `netifrc`, `rc-service net.eth0 status` reports service state.

- `udev` **Debugging:** Enable verbose logging with `udevadm monitor --property` during interface events to validate rule application.

- **DHCP Diagnostics:** Analyzing DHCP client logs (e.g., `/var/log/messages` or `journalctl`) reveals lease issues or server communication problems.

Persistent interface name conflicts can be resolved by cleaning residual `udev` rules and checking `/etc/machine-id` consistency.

Automation Strategies for Rapid Setup

Automation of network interface provisioning accelerates deployment in environments ranging from embedded systems to large-scale datacenters. Common techniques include:

- **Templated Configuration Files:** Utilizing configuration management tools (Ansible, Puppet, etc.) to deploy unified `netifrc` or `udev` rules across machines.

- **Dynamic** `udev` **Rule Generation:** Scripts generate rules based on hardware inventory, ensuring consistent naming without manual intervention.

- **Service Hooks and Scripts:** Custom scripts invoked during interface bring-up or tear-down automate supplementary tasks such as firewall reloading or link monitoring.

- **Preseeded DHCP Clients:** Pre-configured DHCP client behavior can standardize address acquisition and renewal, integrating with network orchestration systems.

A concise `netifrc` automation shell snippet to enable DHCP on all detected Ethernet interfaces might be:

```
for iface in $(ip -o link show | awk -F': ' '{print $2}'
    | grep '^eth'); do
    echo "config_${iface}=dhcp" >> /etc/conf.d/net
    rc-update add net.${iface} default
done
```

This loop ensures all `eth*` interfaces receive DHCP configurations and are enabled in the default runlevel, streamlining provisioning for multi-interface systems.

Network interface provisioning integrates careful interface naming, addressing, and fine-tuning, supported by robust tooling such as `udev` and `netifrc`. Mastery of both static and dynamic configuration modes, combined with advanced tuning techniques and structured troubleshooting, empowers efficient, predictable network deployments. Employing automation extends these benefits at scale, ensuring consistent, rapid network readiness in diverse system environments.

5.2.   Routing, VLANs, and Advanced Networking

The construction of sophisticated network topologies necessitates a comprehensive understanding of routing mechanisms, bridging, link aggregation techniques, multi-homing strategies, and VLAN segmentation. These elements collectively enhance network performance, scalability, and fault tolerance across complex multi-interface environments.

Routing-the process of determining optimal paths for data packets to traverse diverse network segments-is foundational to inter-network communication. Static routing involves manually configured routing entries maintained by network administrators. While simple and predictable, static routes lack adaptability to topology changes, making them suitable only for small, stable networks or backup paths.

Dynamic routing protocols facilitate automatic route discovery and adaptation to network changes through periodic information exchange among routers. Key examples include Routing Information Protocol (RIP), Open Shortest Path First (OSPF), and Border Gateway Protocol (BGP). OSPF, a link-state protocol, offers fast convergence and scalability for intra-domain routing, utilizing Dijkstra's algorithm to compute shortest paths based on link costs. BGP governs inter-domain routing, enabling policy-driven path selection across autonomous systems.

Integration of static and dynamic routes arises in advanced topologies to optimize routing efficiency and control. For example, static default routes may serve as fallbacks in an OSPF environment, while policy-based routing directs traffic through selective interfaces based on predefined criteria.

Bridging connects multiple network segments at Layer 2, transparently forwarding frames based on MAC addresses. This facilitates network expansion without the complexity of routing protocols in small or flat LANs. The Spanning Tree Protocol (STP) is fundamental in bridging configurations to prevent loops and ensure a loop-free topology by selectively blocking redundant paths while maintaining network resilience.

Bridging is particularly beneficial for segment aggregation

and isolating broadcast domains within VLAN implementations. However, bridging alone does not scale well in large, segmented networks due to broadcast traffic propagation and security concerns.

To improve throughput and fault tolerance, multiple physical network interfaces can be combined into a single logical link through techniques known as bonding or link aggregation. The IEEE 802.3ad standard (now 802.1AX) defines Link Aggregation Control Protocol (LACP), allowing dynamic negotiation of link bundles between switches or hosts.

Bonding modes commonly include:

- **Active-Backup**: Only one interface is active; others serve as failover links, ensuring continuous availability with no load balancing.

- **Adaptive Load Balancing**: Distributes traffic across available interfaces based on load or hashing algorithms, enhancing throughput.

- **LACP Aggregation**: Actively negotiates aggregation groups with compatible peers to maximize bandwidth and provide redundancy.

Best practices in bonding mandate matching interface speeds, consistent duplex settings, and compatible switch support. Monitoring link states and employing link aggregation across diverse switch ports prevent single points of failure.

Multi-homing involves connecting a network or device to multiple ISPs or network segments to increase reliability and improve load distribution. This setup requires robust routing configurations to handle path failover and avoid routing loops.

In practice, multi-homing applies both at Layer 3 and Layer 2. At Layer 3, techniques like BGP multi-homing use path attributes and policy enforcement to select optimal routes, enabling automatic rerouting upon link failures. For smaller scales, policy-based routing and source-based routing provide granular control over outbound traffic paths.

Link diversity and independent physical paths are essential to realize the full benefits, minimizing correlated failures. Multi-homed hosts may also employ multipath TCP (MPTCP) to simultaneously utilize multiple interfaces for improved throughput and resilience.

Virtual Local Area Networks (VLANs) permit logical segmentation of a single physical network into multiple isolated broadcast domains. VLAN tagging, specified in IEEE 802.1Q, inserts a VLAN identifier into Ethernet frames to demarcate traffic belonging to different logical networks.

Segmentation via VLANs offers several advantages:

- **Security**: Traffic isolation reduces exposure to unauthorized devices and limits broadcast domains.

- **Performance**: Smaller broadcast domains decrease unnecessary traffic, improving overall efficiency.

- **Management**: Simplifies network organization by grouping users and resources logically rather than physically.

Trunk ports carry multiple VLANs between switches, preserving tags for end-to-end segregation. Access ports terminate VLAN membership for connected hosts, untagging frames for compatibility.

Inter-VLAN routing enables communication across VLANs, typically implemented on Layer 3 devices using router-on-a-stick configurations or multi-layer switches. Proper design requires careful consideration of IP addressing schemes, ACLs, and routing policies to maintain segregation and control traffic flow.

In multi-interface setups combining routing, VLANs, and bonding, several best practices enhance network robustness:

- **Consistent Configuration**: Synchronize VLAN tagging, interface modes, and routing policies across all devices.

- **Redundant Paths**: Deploy multiple physical and logical links that can seamlessly take over upon failure.

- **Monitoring and Alerts**: Incorporate real-time status checks on interface states, link aggregation health, and routing protocol metrics.

- **Load Balancing**: Employ traffic distribution techniques to prevent interface saturation without causing packet reordering.

- **Separation of Control and Data Planes**: Design networks to ensure that routing control messages remain reliable even under data plane congestion.

Advanced networking demands a balanced approach encompassing both architectural design and operational discipline to maintain high availability, scalable performance, and secure segmentation across evolving environments.

5.3. Firewalling with nftables and iptables

Modern Linux-based firewalls rely heavily on two principal tools: `iptables` and `nftables`. Both serve to configure packet filtering, network address translation (NAT), and port forwarding, yet they differ in design philosophy, syntax, and extensibility. Understanding these systems and how to build flexible, scriptable firewalls using them is critical for crafting environments that can adapt fluidly across development and production use cases.

Both `iptables` and `nftables` operate on packet filtering rules organized into tables and chains. These chains correspond to hooks in the Linux kernel networking stack-most notably INPUT, OUTPUT, and FORWARD-where rules inspect packets based on source, destination, protocols, and interfaces.

Under `iptables`, filtering rules are managed per table-such as `filter` for basic filtering, `nat` for translation, and `mangle` for specialized packet alterations. Rule processing is sequential; the first matching rule with an explicit target (e.g., ACCEPT, DROP) determines the fate of the packet.

In contrast, `nftables` employs a single matching engine and a consolidated rule space with reduced redundancy. It supports sets and maps for efficient matching, as well as expressions allowing more complex conditionals and a stateful approach to rule evaluation.

Implementing NAT is fundamental for scenarios where internal private IP address spaces must communicate over public networks. `iptables` uses the `nat` table, with chains like PREROUTING (for DNAT) and POSTROUTING (for SNAT or MASQUERADE).

A typical use case is port forwarding, redirecting external traffic on a public interface to a specific internal host
and port. Consider forwarding TCP port 8080 on the
external interface eth0 to port 80 on an internal server
192.168.1.100:

```
iptables -t nat -A PREROUTING -i eth0 -p tcp --dport
    8080 -j DNAT --to-destination 192.168.1.100:80
iptables -t nat -A POSTROUTING -o eth1 -j MASQUERADE
```

Here, the PREROUTING rule performs Destination NAT
(DNAT) to redirect packets, and POSTROUTING applies
source address masquerading for outbound traffic.

In nftables, this is expressed more succinctly using the
concatenated configuration syntax with tables and chains:

```
table ip nat {
    chain prerouting {
        type nat hook prerouting priority 0;
        iif "eth0" tcp dport 8080 dnat to
        192.168.1.100:80
    }
    chain postrouting {
        type nat hook postrouting priority 100;
        oif "eth1" masquerade
    }
}
```

This approach tightly integrates NAT rules and leverages
priorities to ensure proper timing of the hooks. The use of
iif (input interface) and oif (output interface) selectors
enables precise targeting.

The construction of robust firewalls mandates the ability
to script rule deployment, rollback, and dynamic updates.
Both iptables and nftables have mature command-line
interfaces facilitating this, but nftables excels with its native transactional updates and atomic commit model.

In iptables, rule manipulation is primarily linear, with
the potential risk of incomplete or inconsistent states during live updates. Scripts customarily flush chains before

reapplying rules:

```
iptables -F
iptables -t nat -F
iptables -A INPUT -m state --state ESTABLISHED,RELATED -
    j ACCEPT
iptables -A INPUT -p tcp --dport 22 -j ACCEPT
iptables -A INPUT -j DROP
```

While effective, this can lead to transient connection drops. Conversely, nftables allows transactional batch loading of an entire ruleset:

```
nft -f /etc/nftables.conf
```

Where /etc/nftables.conf contains the full set of rules defining tables, chains, and policies. This entire configuration is parsed and committed atomically, reducing race conditions and maintaining stability during rule changes.

An advanced firewall design separates concerns by layering rulesets to accommodate distinct operational requirements. Development environments often require permissive rules with extensive logging and debugging facilities, while production systems demand strict, minimal attack surface exposure with fail-safe defaults.

A layered approach can combine mangle, filter, and nat tables, alongside user-defined chains for clarity and modularity. For instance, a base policy chain enforces high-level access controls, while secondary chains govern specific service or interface-level rules.

Using nftables's set abstraction facilitates efficient grouping:

```
table inet filter {
    set allowed_ssh_ips {
        type ipv4_addr
        elements = { 192.168.1.10, 10.0.0.2 }
    }
    chain input {
        type filter hook input priority 0;
        policy drop;
```

117

```
        ct state established,related accept;
        ip saddr @allowed_ssh_ips tcp dport 22 accept;
        counter log prefix "Dropped packet: " drop;
    }
}
```

This design uses a set `allowed_ssh_ips` for source address whitelisting on SSH access. The `counter` and `log` elements enable tight observability on rejected traffic, helping developers monitor unanticipated access attempts during testing without compromising production stability.

When layering firewall rules, it is essential to maintain a default-deny stance, explicitly specifying allowances rather than exceptions. Both `iptables` and `nftables` advocate for minimal exposure surfaces: rules should be as narrow as possible with respect to source IPs, destination ports, and protocols.

Furthermore, harnessing connection tracking modules (`conntrack`) reduces state inspection complexity and prevents common attack vectors such as spoofing or session hijacking. Rules incorporating `-m state --state ESTABLISHED,RELATED` or `ct state` significantly reduce manual rule complexity and improve operational reliability.

For development environments, incorporating verbose logging and selective ACCEPT policies accelerates troubleshooting, but these must be carefully removed or adjusted prior to deployment to avoid information leakage or unnecessary resource consumption.

Despite `nftables` being the modern replacement, many legacy systems and scripts continue to leverage `iptables`. Linux supports coexistence via compatibility layers allowing `iptables`-type commands to interact with `nftables` backends or the `xt_ables` modules.

Transitioning from `iptables` to `nftables` can be facilitated by tools like `iptables-translate`, which converts `iptables` rules into `nftables` syntax:

```
iptables-translate -A INPUT -p tcp --dport 80 -j ACCEPT
```

Outputs:

```
add rule ip filter INPUT tcp dport 80 accept
```

Leveraging this smooths integration and modernization efforts, allowing for incremental migrations without wholesale disruptions.

Strategic firewalling with `nftables` and `iptables` combines fine-grained control over NAT, port forwarding, and packet filtering with the flexibility of scripting and modular rule layering. Mastery of these tools enables technical users to implement security postures tailored to both experimental development and hardened production environments, ensuring resilience while maintaining agility at scale.

5.4. VPNs and Encrypted Networking

Virtual Private Networks (VPNs) enable secure communication across untrusted networks by establishing encrypted tunnels between endpoints. Deploying VPNs correctly is essential for protecting data integrity, confidentiality, and authentication in corporate environments, remote access, and site-to-site connectivity. This section details the practical deployment of secure VPN solutions-specifically WireGuard, OpenVPN, and strongSwan for IPsec-illustrating how to safeguard communications between diverse sites, users, and devices.

WireGuard Deployment

WireGuard is a modern VPN protocol emphasizing simplicity, high performance, and strong cryptography. It operates within the Linux kernel and supports multiple platforms. WireGuard requires minimal configuration compared to traditional VPNs.

1. **Key Generation**: Each peer must generate a private and public key pair.

```
wg genkey | tee privatekey | wg pubkey > publickey
```

2. **Peer Configuration**: Configure each peer's interface with its private key, assign a unique IP address within the VPN subnet (e.g., 10.0.0.1/24), and specify the peers it will communicate with through their public keys and allowed IP ranges.

```
[Interface]
PrivateKey = <peer_private_key>
Address = 10.0.0.1/24
ListenPort = 51820

[Peer]
PublicKey = <remote_peer_public_key>
AllowedIPs = 10.0.0.2/32
Endpoint = remote.example.com:51820
PersistentKeepalive = 25
```

3. **Firewall Rules and IP Forwarding**: Enable IP forwarding on Linux to allow routing between interfaces:

```
sysctl -w net.ipv4.ip_forward=1
```

Set firewall rules permitting traffic on WireGuard's UDP port (default 51820):

```
iptables -A INPUT -p udp --dport 51820 -j ACCEPT
iptables -A FORWARD -i wg0 -j ACCEPT
iptables -A FORWARD -o wg0 -j ACCEPT
```

4. **Interface Activation**: Bring up the WireGuard interface:

```
wg-quick up wg0
```

WireGuard's performance benefits come from its streamlined cryptographic primitives (Curve25519 for key exchange, ChaCha20 for symmetric encryption) and its simple yet secure handshake model.

OpenVPN Setup

OpenVPN is a widely-supported SSL/TLS-based VPN solution, flexible for various topologies and encryption algorithms. Its maturity provides robust authentication and extensive configuration capabilities.

1. **Public Key Infrastructure (PKI) Setup**: Generate a Certificate Authority (CA), server certificate, and client certificates using easy-rsa or openssl.

```
./easyrsa init-pki
./easyrsa build-ca nopass
./easyrsa gen-req server nopass
./easyrsa sign-req server server
./easyrsa gen-req client1 nopass
./easyrsa sign-req client client1
```

2. **Server Configuration**: An example snippet of typical server.conf:

```
port 1194
proto udp
dev tun
ca ca.crt
cert server.crt
key server.key
dh dh.pem
server 10.8.0.0 255.255.255.0
push "redirect-gateway def1 bypass-dhcp"
push "dhcp-option DNS 8.8.8.8"
keepalive 10 120
cipher AES-256-CBC
auth SHA256
user nobody
group nogroup
persist-key
```

```
persist-tun
status openvpn-status.log
verb 3
```

3. **Client Configuration**: The client requires the CA certificate along with its own certificate and key. A minimal client config:

```
client
dev tun
proto udp
remote vpn.example.com 1194
resolv-retry infinite
nobind
persist-key
persist-tun
cipher AES-256-CBC
auth SHA256
remote-cert-tls server
<ca>
-----BEGIN CERTIFICATE-----
...
-----END CERTIFICATE-----
</ca>
<cert>
-----BEGIN CERTIFICATE-----
...
-----END CERTIFICATE-----
</cert>
<key>
-----BEGIN PRIVATE KEY-----
...
-----END PRIVATE KEY-----
</key>
verb 3
```

4. **Routing and Firewall**: Enable IP forwarding on the server and configure firewall/NAT rules (e.g., using `iptables`) to allow traffic forwarding between the VPN interface and external networks.

```
sysctl -w net.ipv4.ip_forward=1
iptables -t nat -A POSTROUTING -s 10.8.0.0/24 -o
    eth0 -j MASQUERADE
iptables -A INPUT -p udp --dport 1194 -j ACCEPT
iptables -A FORWARD -s 10.8.0.0/24 -j ACCEPT
iptables -A FORWARD -d 10.8.0.0/24 -j ACCEPT
```

5. **Starting the OpenVPN Service**:

```
systemctl start openvpn@server
```

OpenVPN supports TLS authentication, certificate revocation lists, compression options, and tun/tap devices for layer 3 or layer 2 tunneling.

strongSwan for IPsec VPN

strongSwan is a comprehensive IPsec implementation for secure site-to-site or remote access VPNs, relying on standardized protocols such as IKEv2 and leveraging robust cryptographic suites.

1. **Certificate Generation**: Use `ipsec pki` tools or external CAs to create private keys and certificates for the gateways:
```
ipsec pki --gen --outform pem > caKey.pem
ipsec pki --self --ca --in caKey.pem --dn "CN=VPN
    CA" --outform pem > caCert.pem
ipsec pki --gen --outform pem > gwKey.pem
ipsec pki --pub --in gwKey.pem | ipsec pki --issue
    --cacert caCert.pem --cakey caKey.pem --dn "
    CN=gateway1" --san "gateway1" --flag
    serverAuth --flag ikeIntermediate --outform
    pem > gwCert.pem
```

2. **IPsec Configuration File** `ipsec.conf` snippet for site-to-site VPN:
```
config setup
    charondebug="ike 2, knl 2, cfg 2"

conn %default
    keyexchange=ikev2
    ike=aes256-sha2_256-modp2048
    esp=aes256-sha2_256
    dpdaction=clear
    dpddelay=300s
    rekey=yes

conn site-to-site
    left=%defaultroute
    leftid=@gateway1
    leftcert=gwCert.pem
```

```
leftsubnet=10.1.1.0/24
right=198.51.100.2
rightid=@gateway2
rightsubnet=10.2.2.0/24
auto=add
```

3. **Authentication Credentials**: Use the `ipsec.secrets` file to point to private keys:

```
: RSA gwKey.pem
```

4. **Starting strongSwan**: Initiate and enable the IPsec service:

```
ipsec restart
ipsec statusall
```

5. **Firewall Adjustments**: Ensure UDP ports 500 (IKE) and 4500 (NAT-T) and ESP protocol are permitted:

```
iptables -A INPUT -p udp --dport 500 -j ACCEPT
iptables -A INPUT -p udp --dport 4500 -j ACCEPT
iptables -A INPUT -p esp -j ACCEPT
iptables -A INPUT -p ah -j ACCEPT
```

strongSwan supports advanced features such as MO-BIKE for roaming clients, EAP authentication for user credentials, and integration with existing PKI infrastructures.

Interoperability and Use Cases

All three VPN solutions can be tailored for multiple scenarios:

- **Remote Access**: OpenVPN and strongSwan with IKEv2 support flexible authentication (certificates, username/password), useful for mobile or teleworker access.

124

- **Site-to-Site**: strongSwan's IPsec and WireGuard's routing capabilities enable high-performance encrypted tunnels between corporate branches.

- **Device-to-Device**: WireGuard's efficient key management suits peer-to-peer encrypted communication in constrained environments.

Each protocol's cryptographic design must be carefully matched with organizational security policies, performance requirements, and existing infrastructure. Network address translation (NAT), multi-homing, firewall policies, and compliance considerations must be included during design and deployment.

Successful deployment requires attention to logging and monitoring the VPN lifecycle, including handshake failures, tunnel status, and traffic throughput. Integrating with automated configuration management and orchestration tools can streamline scaling to multiple sites and users without compromising security.

The balance between simplicity and cryptographic robustness positions WireGuard as the protocol of choice for many modern deployments, while OpenVPN and strongSwan remain indispensable for environments requiring complex configurations, legacy compatibility, or specialized authentication workflows.

5.5. Intrusion Detection, Monitoring, and Response

Intrusion detection and network monitoring constitute cornerstone components of contemporary cybersecurity architectures, enabling the identification, alerting, and mitigation of malicious activities. The deployment of tools such as Suricata, Snort, and fail2ban, combined with effective tuning and response strategies, facilitates early threat detection and automated defense mechanisms essential for maintaining system integrity.

Suricata and Snort operate as highly versatile network intrusion detection and prevention systems (NIDS/NIPS), employing signature-based, protocol-aware inspection to scrutinize incoming and outgoing network traffic. Both tools rely on comprehensive rule sets to match known attack patterns, while also supporting anomaly and heuristic detection to enhance adaptive security coverage. The deployment of Suricata or Snort typically involves the insertion of these sensors at strategic points within the network, such as network perimeters, data center ingress/egress points, and critical server segments, to provide layered visibility.

Configuration and tuning of Suricata and Snort demand meticulous attention to performance and accuracy trade-offs. Initial deployment should focus on tailoring rule sets to the specific network environment. Utilizing vendor-maintained and community-curated rule repositories like Emerging Threats or the Snort Subscriber Rules enhances detection fidelity. However, indiscriminate application of all available rules may lead to elevated false positive rates and resource exhaustion. Practical tuning involves iterative rule selection based on observed network baselines and traffic profiles.

Essential configuration parameters include stream reassembly options, protocol detection thresholds, and flow timeout values. For instance, fine-tuning TCP stream reassembly parameters in Suricata can improve detection of evasion attempts employing segmentation and fragmentation techniques. Additionally, enabling HTTP parsing and DNS inspection modules provides deeper packet insight essential for detecting application-layer attacks.

Fail2ban functions as a host-based intrusion prevention tool that monitors log files generated by various services (SSH, web servers, mail servers) to identify suspicious activity patterns, primarily brute-force attempts and automated exploitation. By tracking authentication failures and suspicious command executions, fail2ban dynamically updates firewall rules to temporarily or permanently ban offending IP addresses, thus slowing or halting attack progression.

The practical integration of fail2ban involves specifying the jail configurations that define which log files to monitor, the regex patterns to apply, and the ban action parameters such as ban time, find time, and maximum retries. Tuning fail2ban requires calibrating these parameters to balance security rigor and user convenience, minimizing the risk of false bans while ensuring aggressive blocking of repeated offenders.

Combining Suricata or Snort with fail2ban allows for a multi-layered defense-in-depth strategy. Network-wide anomalous traffic alerts generated by Suricata or Snort can trigger broader incident response workflows, while fail2ban provides immediate reactive controls at the host level. Furthermore, integration through centralized logging and analysis platforms (e.g., Security Information and Event Management-SIEM-systems) enhances correlation and forensic capabilities.

To illustrate a practical tactic, consider deployment on a Linux-based perimeter firewall. Suricata is installed with an initial tailored rule set focused on protocols prevalent in the environment (e.g., HTTP, SMTP, DNS). Logging output is directed to a central log management system using the JSON format to facilitate automated parsing. Fail2ban is configured with a jail monitoring the Suricata alert log files, employing regular expressions to detect repeated signature matches from the same IP address, thus creating dynamic IP banning based on network threat activity.

Effective early threat detection mandates continuous tuning driven by threat intelligence and operational analysis. Initial alarm thresholds should be conservative, reducing alert fatigue, with gradual adjustment in response to actual attack trends and network behavior deviations. Automated alerting integrates with incident response platforms via syslog forwarding, SNMP traps, or email notifications to enable prompt analyst action.

A conceptual example of a minimal fail2ban jail configuration tuned to monitor SSH authentication failures follows:

```
[sshd]
enabled  = true
filter   = sshd
logpath  = /var/log/auth.log
maxretry = 5
findtime = 600
bantime  = 3600
```

Here, `maxretry` sets the number of allowed failed login attempts before banning, `findtime` specifies the observation window in seconds (10 minutes), and `bantime` defines the duration of the IP ban (1 hour). Such parameters can be modified based on observed login patterns and threat severity.

Suricata's startup command with specified configuration file and logging options can be exemplified as:

```
sudo suricata -c /etc/suricata/suricata.yaml -i eth0 --
    runmode=autofp --unix-socket=/var/run/suricata-
    command.socket
```

This invocation assigns Suricata to interface eth0, uses the specified configuration, enables autofp (automatic failure prevention mode), and provides a command socket interface for runtime control and adjustments.

Automated response can be further enhanced by coupling intrusion detection alerts with orchestration tools such as Ansible or custom scripts that dynamically update firewall rules or quarantine network segments. For example, executing a script upon detection of a high-confidence alert to block malicious IP ranges using iptables or nftables constitutes a rapid mitigation strategy.

Finally, robust logging and monitoring infrastructure is indispensable. Persistent storage of alert logs, correlation with other system logs, and visualization dashboards contribute to maintaining situational awareness and enabling post-incident analysis. Ensuring time synchronization across all monitoring nodes via NTP is critical for accurate event sequencing and troubleshooting.

The deployment, tuning, and orchestration of intrusion detection and response tools must be a continuous, data-driven process. It requires balancing operational constraints with detection sensitivity and response aggressiveness to build a resilient security posture capable of countering evolving and sophisticated cyber threats.

5.6. Network Service Security

Network services such as SSH, DNS, and web proxies form critical components of modern infrastructure; however, their ubiquitous exposure inherently expands the attack surface. Hardening these services is fundamental to safeguarding against exploitation attempts, which often leverage default configurations, known vulnerabilities, or improper deployment practices. Effective hardening combines disciplined configuration management, proactive attack mitigation techniques, and continuous minimization of service exposure.

Secure Shell (SSH)

SSH remains the cornerstone for secure remote administration, making it a high-value target. By default, SSH servers accept connections using password authentication and broad compatibility options, increasing susceptibility to brute-force and credential-stuffing attacks.

Best practices for SSH hardening include:

- **Disabling Password Authentication:** Enforcing public key authentication forces attackers to bypass weak or stolen passwords. This is configured by setting `PasswordAuthentication no` in `sshd_config`.

- **Restricting Access by User and Host:** Limiting login to specific users or groups via `AllowUsers` or `AllowGroups` reduces unnecessary exposure. Network-level ACLs can further restrict client source IPs.

- **Changing the Default Port:** While not a security measure by itself, moving SSH off port 22 reduces noise from automated scans and bots.

- **Limiting Authentication Methods:** Disabling less secure options such as `ChallengeResponseAuthentication` and `KerberosAuthentication` lowers risk profiles.

- **Enabling Rate Limiting and Fail2Ban:** Integrating intrusion prevention tools to dynamically block IPs after failed attempts mitigates brute-force threats.

```
Port 2222
PermitRootLogin no
PasswordAuthentication no
ChallengeResponseAuthentication no
UsePAM yes
AllowUsers admin user1
LoginGraceTime 30
MaxAuthTries 3
```

These configurations narrow the login vector while preserving operational flexibility. Additionally, enforcing protocol version 2 exclusively (default in modern SSH) guards against weaknesses in older implementations.

Domain Name System (DNS)

DNS infrastructure stands as a high-value target due to its fundamental role in name resolution and internet traffic routing. DNS servers, especially authoritative and recursive resolvers exposed on the public internet, are vulnerable to cache poisoning, amplification attacks, and zone transfer exploits.

Hardened DNS configurations should encompass:

- **Segregation of Recursive and Authoritative Services:** Recursive resolvers should not serve authoritative zones to prevent cache pollution.

- **Rate Limiting DNS Queries:** Settings to limit the number of UDP or TCP queries per client reduce amplification attack potential.

- **Implementing DNSSEC Validation:** Signing zones and enabling validation prevents spoofed or tampered responses, protecting integrity.

- **Restricting Zone Transfers:** Zone transfers

should be limited to trusted IP addresses via `allow-transfer` directives.

- **Disabling Recursive Queries for External Clients:** Recursive lookup should be restricted to internal or authenticated clients to prevent abuse.

```
options {
    recursion no;
    allow-query { any; };
    allow-transfer { 192.168.1.10; };
    rate-limit {
        responses-per-second 5;
    };
    dnssec-validation auto;
};
```

Adequate monitoring of query logs can detect unusual request patterns characteristic of amplification or cache poisoning attempts. Deploying dedicated DNS firewalls and leveraging Response Policy Zones (RPZ) augment the defense-in-depth posture.

Web Proxies

Web proxies serve multiple roles including content filtering, performance optimization, and anonymity. Their position as intermediaries between clients and external sites makes them targets for injection attacks, misconfiguration exploitation, and session hijacking.

Effective hardening measures include:

- **Access Controls:** Enforce granular authentication mechanisms such as Kerberos or client certificates to prevent unauthorized use.

- **Cache Management:** Proper handling of HTTP headers such as `Cache-Control` and `Pragma` prevents sensitive data leakage through caching.

- **HTTPS Interception Security:** When SSL bumping is enabled, managing trusted certificate authorities and safeguarding private keys avoids man-in-the-middle vulnerabilities.

- **Logging and Anomaly Detection:** Detailed request and response logging enables swift identification of abusive patterns or attack attempts.

- **Regular Software Updates and Patch Management:** Web proxy software often targets well-understood vulnerabilities; maintaining currency prevents exploitation.

```
http_port 3128 ssl-bump generate-host-certificates=on
    dynamic_cert_mem_cache_size=4MB
acl allowed_users proxy_auth REQUIRED
http_access allow allowed_users
ssl_bump peek step1 all
ssl_bump splice all
cache deny QUERY
via off
forwarded_for delete
header_access X-Forwarded-For deny all
```

Minimizing open ports and running proxies with non-privileged accounts further reduces risk. Limiting listening interfaces specifically to trusted networks or VPNs constricts exposure footprints.

Maintaining Minimal Attack Surfaces

A unifying principle across all network services is the continuous effort to minimize the exposed attack surface. This entails:

- **Principle of Least Privilege:** Running services with minimum necessary permissions restricts potential damage from successful exploits.

- **Disabling Unused Features:** Every protocol extension, module, or metadata leakage vector turned

133

off reduces exploitable functionality.

- **Service Exposure Audit and Segmentation:** Routine audits paired with network segmentation, VLANs, and firewall rules keep services reachable only by necessary peers.

- **Automated Configuration Management:** Using automation frameworks ensures consistency and rapid deployment of hardening policies.

Real-world mitigations must consider evolving threat landscapes. For instance, SSH brute-force botnets adapt to port changes and disabled password login by targeting poorly managed keys or exploiting configuration drifts. DNS amplification remains a primary denial-of-service vector, necessitating adaptive rate limiting and presence detection. Similarly, web proxy misconfigurations continue to permit unauthorized access or bypass content restrictions when logging or ACLs are incomplete.

Achieving robust network service security is a multi-faceted endeavor requiring strategic configuration decisions, operational vigilance, and a commitment to maintaining minimal, well-monitored exposure surfaces. The synergy of well-targeted hardening measures and proactive threat response ensures essential network services provide both functionality and resilience under adversarial conditions.

Chapter 6

Running and Securing Network Services

The heart of digital infrastructure lies in the network services we deploy and defend. On Alpine Linux, you have the power not only to run lean, high-performance server workloads, but also to lock them down with modern, automated security. Journey through this chapter to discover how to configure, scale, and harden essential services— ensuring every HTTP request, database transaction, and email message is fast, reliable, and impenetrably secure.

6.1. HTTP/HTTPS Service Stacks

The deployment of HTTP/HTTPS service stacks is a critical aspect of modern web infrastructure, directly impacting performance, scalability, and security. This section

delves into the deployment, fine-tuning, and security hardening of popular web servers, namely nginx, Apache, and
Caddy. A comprehensive understanding of these components enables robust service delivery through effective
load balancing, reverse proxying, Transport Layer Security (TLS) configuration, and automation of routine maintenance tasks.

Deployment and Configuration

Each web server technology embodies distinct architectural philosophies and configuration paradigms. nginx
is designed primarily as an event-driven asynchronous
server, excelling in concurrency and static content delivery. Apache, historically rooted in a process-based model,
provides extensive module support and configurability
through its multiprocess or multiprocess-threaded modes
(e.g., prefork, worker, and event). Caddy emphasizes automatic HTTPS and simplicity in configuration, leveraging
Go-based architecture.

Deployment begins with establishing an accurate configuration that balances server resource usage and expected
traffic. For nginx, configuration files are organized
under /etc/nginx/, where the nginx.conf governs core
directives and the sites-available/sites-enabled
scheme manages virtual hosts. Apache settings reside
within httpd.conf or modularized configuration files
under sites-available/, utilizing .htaccess for
directory-level control where enabled. Caddy uses a
singular Caddyfile, emphasizing declarative syntax
streamlined for HTTPS.

Fine-Tuning and Performance Optimization

Fine-tuning the service stack enhances throughput,
latency, and resilience under load. Key parameters

include worker processes/threads, connection timeouts, buffer sizes, and caching mechanisms. For nginx, adjusting the worker_processes to match available CPU cores is fundamental for parallelism. Connection handling is governed by directives like worker_connections, which define concurrent clients per worker process. Buffer optimizations include tuning client_body_buffer_size and various cache controls with the proxy_cache mechanism for reverse proxy scenarios.

Apache requires careful selection of Multi-Processing Modules (MPMs) suited to the workload. The event MPM leverages asynchronous connection handling, reducing memory per connection relative to prefork. Cache modules such as mod_cache and mod_expires further optimize delivery of static and dynamically generated content. Thread and connection timeouts avoid resource exhaustion under slow client conditions.

Caddy abstracts much of the tuning but offers explicit control over graceful shutdown time and request timeouts in its configuration. Given its design focus on automation, explicit caching and worker tuning are less prominent but can be customized using plugin modules and environment variables.

Load Balancing and Reverse Proxying

Load balancing distributes incoming traffic across back-end servers to improve availability and throughput. Both nginx and Apache feature native modules supporting reverse proxy load balancing, while Caddy integrates this capability with automatic TLS.

In nginx, the upstream directive defines backend pools, with load balancing algorithms including round-robin (default), least_connections, and ip_hash, facilitating session affinity. Health checks and failover mechanisms can be implemented using the max_fails and fail_timeout options. An example snippet configuring an upstream block is:

```
upstream backend_pool {
    server backend1.example.com weight=5;
    server backend2.example.com max_fails=3 fail_timeout
    =30s;
    least_conn;
}
server {
    listen 80;
    location / {
        proxy_pass http://backend_pool;
        proxy_set_header Host $host;
        proxy_set_header X-Real-IP $remote_addr;
    }
}
```

Apache implements load balancing via the mod_proxy_balancer module. Backend members are defined within a <Proxy> block, where session persistence is configurable using stickiness methods like cookies. Failover and load distribution are similarly adjustable.

Caddy simplifies reverse proxy configuration and balances load by listing multiple backend servers. Its configuration automatically manages retries and health checks when enabled. The declaration form resembles:

```
:80 {
    reverse_proxy backend1.example.com backend2.example.
    com {
        lb_policy least_conn
        health_path /healthz
        health_interval 10s
    }
}
```

TLS Configuration and Security Hardening

Securing HTTP traffic mandates strong TLS configuration

and rigorous security hardening. Caddy distinguishes itself with built-in automatic HTTPS provisioning using the ACME protocol, simplifying certificate procurement and renewal without manual intervention.

For nginx and Apache, explicit TLS configuration is necessary. Key security best practices include enforcing TLS versions 1.2 and above, disabling weak cipher suites, enabling HTTP Strict Transport Security (HSTS), and utilizing OCSP stapling to reduce client-side certificate validation latency.

An example nginx TLS configuration excerpt enforces a secure profile:

```
server {
    listen 443 ssl http2;
    ssl_certificate /etc/ssl/certs/example.crt;
    ssl_certificate_key /etc/ssl/private/example.key;
    ssl_protocols TLSv1.2 TLSv1.3;
    ssl_ciphers HIGH:!aNULL:!MD5;
    ssl_prefer_server_ciphers on;
    ssl_stapling on;
    ssl_stapling_verify on;
    add_header Strict-Transport-Security "max-age
    =63072000; includeSubDomains" always;
}
```

In Apache, the analogous directives include SSLEngine on, SSLProtocol, SSLCipherSuite, and Header settings for HSTS. Certificate management can be automated using tools like Certbot with integration for mod_ssl.

Hardening extends beyond TLS to incorporate security headers such as Content-Security-Policy, X-Content-Type-Options, and X-Frame-Options to mitigate common web vulnerabilities. Rate limiting, IP filtering, and Web Application Firewall (WAF) integration reinforce perimeter defense. Enabling logging with rich detail facilitates anomaly detection and forensic analysis.

Automation and Routine Maintenance

Automation significantly reduces operational overhead and human error in managing HTTP/HTTPS service stacks. Common maintenance tasks amenable to scripting and orchestration include certificate renewal, configuration validation, log rotation, and backup.

nginx and Apache configurations can be tested non-disruptively via:

```
# nginx
nginx -t

# apache
apachectl configtest
```

These commands enable pre-deployment validation in continuous integration pipelines. Certificates acquired via Let's Encrypt are renewed automatically with certbot cron jobs or systemd timers.

Log rotation is typically managed by tools such as logrotate, configured to prevent disk exhaustion and maintain compliance. Automation scripts incorporate graceful service restarts and reloads to apply updates without downtime:

```
# nginx graceful reload
nginx -s reload

# apache graceful restart
apachectl graceful
```

Configuration and infrastructure as code tools, e.g., Ansible, Terraform, or Puppet, contribute to consistent environment replication and auditability. Caddy's design emphasizes minimal manual intervention, with built-in HTTPS certificate lifecycle management and hot-reload capabilities, enhancing automation out of the box.

Summary of Key Configuration Components

Component	Best Practices
Worker Processes and Threads	Align `nginx worker_processes` or Apache MPM with available CPU cores for optimum concurrency.
Connection and Request Timeouts	Set conservative timeouts to safeguard against slow-client attacks and resource starvation.
Reverse Proxy	Use health checks, session affinity, and load balancing algorithms to enhance backend resilience.
TLS Configuration	Enforce TLS 1.2+, disable weak ciphers, enable OCSP stapling and HSTS headers.
Security Headers	Implement CSP, X-Frame-Options, X-Content-Type-Options, and other headers to protect clients.
Automation	Employ configuration validation, certificate auto-renewal, and log management in automated workflows.

Through meticulous deployment, tuning, and security practices, HTTP/HTTPS service stacks can sustain high-demand web applications securely and efficiently. Integrating these technical considerations ensures scalable service delivery aligned with contemporary operational standards.

6.2. Database Engines

Database engines form the backbone of modern applications, necessitating installations that are reliable and optimized for specific workloads. Among prominent options, MariaDB, PostgreSQL, and SQLite serve distinct roles, ranging from enterprise-level clustering to embedded data storage. This section discusses their deployment, configuration for performance, and security considerations tailored to robust backend systems.

MariaDB, a widely deployed fork of MySQL, emphasizes scalability and clustering capabilities. Installation typically involves package management systems on Linux (e.g., apt or yum) or binary distributions for Windows and macOS. Post-installation initialization sets default system tables, after which crucial configuration resides in the my.cnf file:

```
[mysqld]
bind-address=0.0.0.0
max_connections=1000
innodb_buffer_pool_size=2G
query_cache_type=0
skip-name-resolve
```

Key tuning parameters focus on InnoDB, the default storage engine within MariaDB. The innodb_buffer_pool_size governs memory allocation for caching data and indexes, influencing I/O operations and throughput. Setting skip-name-resolve disables DNS hostname resolution, reducing connection overhead in clustered environments.

For high availability and failover, MariaDB supports Galera Cluster, a synchronous multi-master replication setup requiring additional setup of the wsrep provider. Nodes communicate using SST and IST protocols to ensure data consistency and automatic node state synchronization on join or recovery:

```
[mysqld]
wsrep_on=ON
wsrep_cluster_address="gcomm://node1_ip,node2_ip,
    node3_ip"
wsrep_provider=/usr/lib/galera/libgalera_smm.so
wsrep_sst_method=rsync
```

Operational tuning for Galera includes monitoring flow control pauses and adjusting wsrep_slave_threads for parallel applying of replication events. Load balancing proxies like MaxScale or HAProxy frequently mediate client connections to evenly distribute query load and maintain uptime.

PostgreSQL installation affords a modular configuration, facilitated by its postgresql.conf and pg_hba.conf files that respectively control internals and client authentication policies. Especially critical parameters include memory, parallel execution, and checkpoint tuning:

```
shared_buffers = 1GB
work_mem = 64MB
max_parallel_workers_per_gather = 4
checkpoint_completion_target = 0.9
```

The shared_buffers directive allocates memory for caching data pages to mitigate disk I/O. Adjusting work_mem affects sorting and hash operations, directly impacting query performance on complex workloads. PostgreSQL's robust access control model relies on pg_hba.conf, where client authentication methods such as md5, scram-sha-256, or certificate-based verification are selectively applied by IP range, user, and database:

```
# TYPE    DATABASE          USER          ADDRESS
                METHOD
host    all               all           192.168.0.0/24
                scram-sha-256
hostssl replication       repl_user     10.0.0.0/16
                cert
```

Clustering in PostgreSQL largely relies on logical or streaming replication methods paired with external orchestration tools like Patroni or repmgr for leader election and failover automation. Logical replication enables selective table copying and heterogeneous schema support, whereas streaming replication maintains near real-time binary log shipping.

SQLite contrasts sharply as an embedded, serverless engine optimized for local data storage in applications requiring minimal resources. Installation is usually as simple as linking its C library. Despite lacking clustering, its configuration merits focus on journaling modes and cache size for performance:

```
PRAGMA journal_mode=WAL;
PRAGMA synchronous=NORMAL;
PRAGMA cache_size=10000;
```

Write-Ahead Logging (WAL) enhances concurrency by allowing readers and writers simultaneous access without locking the entire database. Setting synchronous to NORMAL reduces disk sync frequency with an acceptable trade-off between durability and performance.

Regarding access control, SQLite itself does not implement user authentication, as file system permissions govern access. Consequently, deployment involves securing the database file within protected system directories and employing encryption extensions where necessary.

Performance tuning across these engines benefits substantially from careful monitoring of query execution plans, disk I/O patterns, and contention metrics. Tools such as EXPLAIN ANALYZE in PostgreSQL or the performance_schema in MariaDB provide granular insights on inefficient index usage or deadlocks. Regular vacuuming and statistics updates prevent query planner regressions.

Robust access control implementations ensure that only authorized principals execute defined operations. Role management with fine-grained privileges, network segmentation, SSL/TLS encryption, and auditing mechanisms collectively contribute to secure database backends capable of scaling horizontally and vertically.

Tailoring installation, configuration, and optimization procedures to the specific database engine and application requirements constructs a resilient, high-performing foundation for modern data-driven systems. MariaDB delivers scalable clustering for OLTP workloads,

PostgreSQL excels in extensibility and concurrency, and SQLite offers a streamlined embedded option-all necessitating judicious tuning and security enforcement for production-grade reliability.

6.3. DNS, DHCP, and Caching

The Domain Name System (DNS) and Dynamic Host Configuration Protocol (DHCP) constitute foundational services in modern IP networks, providing essential mechanisms for name resolution and automated IP address allocation, respectively. Designing resilient DNS and DHCP infrastructures involves careful attention to redundancy, failover capabilities, caching strategies, and security considerations, ensuring high availability and performance of critical network identity systems.

DNS is inherently distributed, employing a hierarchical namespace structure with authoritative servers responsible for specific zones. Implementing resilience begins with deploying multiple authoritative DNS servers per zone to eliminate single points of failure. These servers should be geographically and topologically dispersed when possible, leveraging anycast routing to increase fault tolerance and reduce latency.

A robust DNS infrastructure typically includes:

- **Primary (Master) and Secondary (Slave) Servers**: The primary server manages zone data and propagates updates to secondary servers through zone transfers (AXFR or IXFR). Secondary servers serve queries and maintain synchronized copies of the zone, facilitating load distribution and failover.

- **Caching Recursive Resolvers**: Internal or local recursive resolvers perform recursive queries on behalf of clients, caching results to minimize external DNS query latency and reduce network traffic.

- **Forwarding**: Recursive resolvers may forward queries to upstream resolver services, enhancing performance via trusted recursive caches.

Zone transfers should be secured using mechanisms like Transaction Signatures (TSIG) to authenticate inter-server communications, preventing unauthorized data replication. DNSSEC (DNS Security Extensions) enables the cryptographic validation of DNS data integrity and origin authenticity, crucial to defending against spoofing and cache poisoning attacks.

DHCP automates IP addressing and configuration distribution. For reliability, DHCP servers must avoid a single point of failure, and several architectures can be employed:

- **DHCP Server Clustering**: Deploy multiple DHCP servers synchronized to provide continuous service even if one server fails.

- **Split Scope Configuration**: Divides the IP address pool between two or more DHCP servers, balancing address allocation responsibility and providing fallback capability.

- **DHCP Failover Protocol**: Standardized protocol allowing two DHCP servers to share lease information and coordinate client assignment, ensuring uninterrupted IP address provision.

The DHCP failover protocol operates in two modes—load balancing and hot standby—adjusting behavior based on network demands and available resources. Lease synchronization intervals should be optimized to reduce the risk of conflicting assignments without imposing excessive network overhead.

Effective caching plays a pivotal role in optimizing DNS query resolution speed and DHCP address assignment efficiency:

DNS Caching: Recursive resolvers cache DNS responses for a duration governed by the resource record's Time-To-Live (TTL) value. Correct TTL configuration requires balancing freshness and efficiency—long TTLs reduce query load but risk stale data persistence; short TTLs provide prompt updates at the cost of increased traffic. Additionally, negative caching (caching of failed lookups) conserves resources by preventing repetitive queries for non-existent domains.

Local DNS caching resolvers deployed close to client networks drastically cut down latency and reduce dependency on external authoritative DNS servers, enhancing resilience. Employing multiple DNS caches with coordinated fallback mechanisms ensures continuous name resolution in case of cache or server outages.

DHCP Caching: DHCP clients cache lease information throughout the lease period, permitting uninterrupted network access during lease renewal processes or temporary server unavailability. DHCP relay agents can cache lease data to accelerate client reassignments in segmented networks. Additionally, lease databases on servers must be robustly backed up and synchronized across failover setups to prevent stale or conflicting assignment information.

147

Designing DNS and DHCP services with redundancy and failover capabilities requires:

- **Multiple Instances**: Deploy at least two authoritative DNS servers per zone and two DHCP servers providing overlapping service.

- **Geographical and Network Diversity**: Distribute servers across different physical locations and network segments to avoid correlated failures.

- **Health Monitoring and Automated Failover**: Integrate monitoring solutions with automated reconfiguration or alerts to handle server failures quickly.

- **Load Balancing**: Employ load balancing mechanisms such as DNS anycast, DHCP failover modes, or front-end proxies to distribute client requests uniformly.

In DHCP, configuring complementary address pools prevents IP conflicts during failover, while in DNS, configuring secondary servers to perform zone transfers securely ensures master-slave consistency.

Protecting DNS and DHCP infrastructures is paramount due to their critical role in network identity and connectivity:

- **DNSSEC**: Enforces cryptographic validation of DNS responses, mitigating cache poisoning.

- **Access Control**: Restrict zone transfer permissions and DHCP management interfaces to authorized systems only.

- **Rate Limiting and Traffic Filtering**: Defend against amplification and denial-of-service attacks that exploit DNS and DHCP protocols.

- **Authentication of DHCP Clients**: Use techniques such as DHCP snooping and Dynamic ARP Inspection to prevent IP spoofing and rogue server insertion.

- **Secure Communications**: Protect inter-server communications with TSIG and IPsec tunnels when traversing untrusted networks.

```
key "transfer-key" {
    algorithm hmac-sha256;
    secret "WJbFjxHwKf1s8Wz/jTgGKQ==";
};

zone "example.com" IN {
    type master;
    file "db.example.com";
    allow-transfer { key "transfer-key"; };
};
```

Secondary servers reference the same key for authenticated zone transfers, ensuring only authorized servers receive zone updates.

Synergistic deployment of DNS and DHCP with caching facilitates a layered approach to reliable address and naming services. Incorporating redundancy, failover mechanisms, caching optimizations, and stringent security policies creates a robust network identity system adaptable to diverse operational environments and capable of sustaining high availability requirements.

6.4. Mail and Messaging Servers

The deployment of robust mail and messaging servers is essential for modern communication infrastructure, integrating critical components such as message transfer agents (MTAs), delivery agents, and user access protocols. The combination of Postfix as an MTA and Dovecot as an IMAP server offers a reliable foundation, while lightweight alternatives permit adaptability to constrained environments. The following delineates systematic steps to deploy, scale, and secure these systems, with particular emphasis on anti-spam mechanisms, encryption protocols, and architectural designs for high availability.

Deployment of Postfix and Dovecot

Postfix manages SMTP transactions by receiving, routing, and delivering mail to local and remote destinations. Its modular configuration permits easy integration with spam filtering and encryption layers. Dovecot provides IMAP and POP3 services, enabling efficient mail retrieval and storage management.

Initial deployment involves configuring Postfix's /etc/postfix/main.cf, setting the myhostname, mydomain, myorigin, relayhost, and inet_interfaces parameters. Ensuring proper DNS records-MX, SPF, DKIM, and DMARC-prior to launch is imperative for mail deliverability and authentication.

Dovecot's configuration primarily resides in /etc/dovecot/dovecot.conf and related files. It requires setting the protocols supported (e.g., IMAP), mail location directories (e.g., mail_location = maildir: /Maildir), and authentication databases. Integration with Postfix is achieved by configuring both to share the same user database and potentially utilizing

LMTP for local delivery.

Scaling Mail Infrastructure

Scaling demands consideration of both load distribution and storage efficiency. Horizontal scaling typically involves distributing inbound SMTP load across multiple Postfix instances using DNS MX records with different priority weights. Load balancers or SMTP proxies (such as HAProxy or NGINX with stream module) can be employed to ameliorate ingress traffic, facilitating redundancy and failover.

For the IMAP layer, Dovecot supports clustering through shared file systems or replicated storage solutions (e.g., GlusterFS or Ceph) to maintain consistency across nodes. Alternatively, Dovecot's replication features can synchronize mailboxes between primary and secondary servers, minimizing data loss during failover.

Database-backed user authentication via SQL or LDAP allows centralized account management, which is crucial in larger environments where user data must be consistent across multiple nodes. Caching mechanisms, such as Redis or Memcached, can reduce authentication load and improve response times.

Lightweight MTA and IMAP Alternatives

Lightweight solutions include `ssmtp` or `nullmailer` for MTAs, appropriate where outbound SMTP relay is necessary without full SMTP server complexity. For IMAP, `Courier-IMAP` or `Mailspring`'s backend can serve constrained systems or specialized use-cases.

Such minimalistic servers generally trade off advanced features (like extensive filtering or complex delivery rules) for simplicity and reduced resource consumption. Despite this, they can be enhanced with external components for spam filtering and encryption, following modular design principles.

Anti-Spam and Content Filtering

Spam mitigation is critical to maintain server integrity and user experience. The standard approach integrates Postfix with content filtering services such as SpamAssassin and ClamAV for virus scanning. Postfix can enforce policy checks using `postscreen` and `postfix-policyd` to regulate connections based on sender reputation, greylisting, or throttling.

An exemplary Postfix content filter pipeline can be defined through `master.cf` to route mails through external filtering daemons before final delivery. For instance:

```
smtp      inet  n      -      n      -      -
    smtpd
    -o content_filter=spamfilter:dummy

spamfilter unix -      n      n      -      -
    pipe
    flags=Rq user=filter argv=/usr/bin/spamc
    -f ${sender} -- ${recipient}
```

This approach allows asynchronous spam processing, offloading CPU-intensive operations and reducing SMTP transaction time.

Greylisting works by temporarily rejecting messages from unknown senders, compelling legitimate servers to retry whereas many spam sources discard such messages. Blacklists and whitelists from Realtime Blackhole Lists (RBLs) further enhance filtering granularity.

Encryption and Security

Transport encryption leverages STARTTLS within Postfix and Dovecot, protecting SMTP and IMAP sessions respectively. Certificates should be obtained from trusted CAs or generated through internal PKI using tools such as Let's Encrypt to automate renewals.

The following configuration snippet in Postfix's `main.cf` enables SMTP TLS:

```
smtpd_tls_cert_file=/etc/letsencrypt/live/example.com/
    fullchain.pem
smtpd_tls_key_file=/etc/letsencrypt/live/example.com/
    privkey.pem
smtpd_use_tls=yes
smtpd_tls_auth_only=yes
smtp_tls_security_level=may
smtp_tls_session_cache_database = btree:${data_directory
    }/smtp_scache
```

Dovecot TLS is similarly configured:

```
ssl = required
ssl_cert = </etc/letsencrypt/live/example.com/fullchain.
    pem
ssl_key = </etc/letsencrypt/live/example.com/privkey.pem
```

At-rest encryption of mail storage can be implemented via filesystem-level encryption (e.g., LUKS or eCryptfs) to safeguard sensitive data.

Authentication hardening includes enforcing strong passwords, using SASL in Postfix with Dovecot's authentication backend, and enabling mechanisms like OAuth or two-factor authentication where feasible.

Ensuring High Availability

High availability (HA) designs require redundancy in both network and storage layers. MX records should list multiple mail servers with different priorities to ensure failover. Postfix instances must be configured to accept mail for the domain and relay to internal delivery agents or shared storage.

Dovecot clusters synchronize mailbox data via replication

or shared storage, ensuring client sessions can resume after node failure. Heartbeat and Pacemaker tools provide service monitoring and automatic failover, restarting services or redirecting traffic as necessary.

Database services for authentication should be made highly available through master-slave replication or distributed databases like MariaDB Galera Cluster.

Backups must be integrated into this design, encompassing configuration files, mail storage, and user databases, with periodic testing of restoration procedures to guarantee resilience.

Summary of Best Practices

- Meticulous DNS configuration, including SPF, DKIM, and DMARC, to improve mail trustworthiness.

- Modular deployment integrating Postfix and Dovecot with external filtering and authentication services.

- Load balancing and clustering for scalability and fault tolerance.

- Layered security through Transport Layer Security (TLS), anti-spam filtering, and strong authentication methods.

- Use of lightweight MTAs or IMAP servers in resource-constrained environments, balanced with extensibility considerations.

- Implementation of redundant systems with automated failover to ensure high availability.

This comprehensive framework ensures an enterprise-grade mail and messaging architecture that meets the demands of performance, scalability, security, and reliability.

6.5. Service Supervision Frameworks

Building upon foundational service initialization and management concepts, modern service supervision frameworks extend operational control by embedding advanced orchestration and fault resilience directly into process lifecycles. While OpenRC provides structured initialization and dependency-based service startup, alternative frameworks such as runit and s6 offer enhanced supervision capabilities to meet the demands of complex, high-availability environments. These frameworks implement continuous monitoring, immediate restarts, and fine-grained recovery policies that enable systems to self-heal and maintain operational continuity autonomously.

runit: Minimalist and Robust Supervision

runit is a cross-platform init and service supervision suite designed to be fast, reliable, and straightforward. Its architecture centers on three stages: initialization, service supervision, and process shutdown. Unlike traditional init systems that primarily focus on startup orchestration, runit excels at providing strong guarantees about service health throughout the runtime.

At the core of runit is the runsv daemon, a per-service supervisor that tirelessly monitors the service process. It maintains a simple yet powerful monitoring loop: if the supervised service terminates, runsv restarts it immediately, preventing transient failures from escalating into downtime. This continuous monitoring forms the basis of *fault containment* and *automatic recovery*. The design philosophy of runit promotes modularity-each service is encapsulated as a directory containing executable scripts and configuration files, allowing tailored lifecycle control independent of other services.

The runit supervision tree enforces a hierarchy where the top-level runsvdir manages multiple runsv instances, enabling collective orchestration of multiple services. This tree structure simplifies parallel supervision and streamlines shutdown sequences, ensuring order and predictability. Furthermore, runit supports service dependencies by implementing a custom ordering mechanism, enabling controlled service start and stop sequences that accommodate critical service interrelations.

s6: Flexible and Extensible Supervision Toolkit

Derived from the design principles of runit and daemontools, s6 advances service supervision with additional flexibility and power, suitable for highly complex and distributed service architectures. s6 is built around small, composable programs that collectively form a complete supervision system. Its modular design facilitates detailed control over service lifecycle, logging, and resource constraints.

Unlike simpler supervisors, s6 separates supervision and orchestration concerns. s6-supervise is the core supervisor, launched per service, constantly ensuring process availability and executing user-defined recovery actions. The s6-svscan process oversees multiple s6-supervise instances, creating a dynamic supervision tree that allows hierarchical monitoring, supporting nested service compositions.

A significant contribution of s6 is its extensible event-driven architecture. It supports notification hooks-scripts triggered on service state changes such as start, stop, or failure-enabling flexible integration with external monitoring and management tools. This event mechanism underpins complex recovery policies, such as conditional restarts, fallback procedures, or orchestration commands for dependent services.

s6 also emphasizes deterministic service shutdown and controlled startup sequencing through its service dependency management features, allowing designers to define precise initialization orders with guarantees of service readiness. These capabilities are paramount in large-scale service ecosystems where the order and timing of component availability govern overall system stability.

Self-Healing and Autonomous Recovery in Service Architectures

Service supervision frameworks like runit and s6 fundamentally enable the design of self-healing systems, where failures are treated as signals triggering automatic recovery mechanisms rather than requiring manual intervention. These frameworks allow architects to embed resilience patterns directly into service lifecycles, enhancing fault tolerance and reducing system downtime.

A central principle in self-healing architectures is *failure detection and recovery automation*. Continuous process monitoring detects abnormal termination or health degradation, upon which supervisors invoke immediate restarts or escalate recovery actions. Supervisors can implement configurable restart strategies such as:

- **Exponential backoff retries**, preventing rapid restart loops that may exacerbate system instability.

- **Circuit breaker behavior**, temporarily halting

157

restart attempts for services exhibiting critical failures, allowing time for underlying issues to resolve.

- **Fallback activation**, where alternative service instances or degraded operation modes are initiated to maintain partial functionality.

Service supervision frameworks facilitate *autonomous dependency management*, ensuring that dependent services are restarted or stopped appropriately in response to state changes. For example, if a database service fails and restarts, dependent web services can be automatically restarted to re-establish connections, preserving application integrity.

Moreover, these frameworks contribute to robust *orchestration patterns* by providing fine-grained control over service start and stop sequences, health verification hooks, and runtime configuration reloading. Integration with logging supervisors ensures that failure contexts are captured promptly, aiding in root cause analysis and further improving system reliability.

Example: Implementing a Resilient Service with s6

Consider a scenario where a critical network daemon must be supervised for autonomous recovery. Utilizing s6, the configuration directory might contain the following run script to launch the service:

```
#!/bin/execlineb -P
s6-setuidgid networkuser
exec /usr/local/sbin/networkd --config /etc/networkd.
    conf
```

The finish script can manage clean shutdown behavior or restart policy:

```
#!/bin/sh
```

158

```
# If the service exited with error, wait before restart
if [ "$1" -ne 0 ]; then
  sleep 10
fi
exit 0
```

By leveraging s6-provided event hooks, an administrator can inject custom actions, such as triggering alerts or gracefully managing dependent services when failures occur. The supervisor will automatically restart the daemon unless a permanent failure mode is detected, embodying the self-healing design.

Comparative Insights and Integration Considerations

Both runit and s6 emphasize simplicity, reliability, and speed but differ in extensibility and sophistication. runit is well suited for environments requiring minimal dependencies and straightforward supervision models. In contrast, s6 accommodates complex supervision scenarios with advanced event management and modular components, at the cost of increased configuration complexity.

When integrating these frameworks into broader operational stacks, compatibility with container orchestration systems, logging infrastructures, and configuration management should be considered. They can complement container supervisors by controlling in-container processes or serve as the init system on lightweight virtual machine images where full-fledged container runtimes are unavailable.

Incorporating these supervision frameworks into service-oriented architectures enhances operational resilience, expedites failure recovery, and facilitates building autonomous distributed systems where fault tolerance is engineered as a first-class attribute of service lifecycle management.

6.6. TLS Certificates and Automated Management

Transport Layer Security (TLS) certificates are indispensable for securing communications over untrusted networks. The management of TLS/SSL certificates has evolved significantly, driven by the need for heightened security, operational efficiency, and compliance with modern cryptographic standards. Contemporary strategies emphasize automation, integration with dynamic certificate authorities, and robust monitoring frameworks to ensure continuous trustworthiness and minimal human intervention.

A pivotal advancement in TLS certificate management is the widespread adoption of Let's Encrypt, a certificate authority that provides free, automated, and domain-validated certificates. Its integration leverages the Automated Certificate Management Environment (ACME) protocol, which defines a standardized communication mechanism between certificate authorities and clients for certificate issuance and renewal. This automation drastically reduces administrative overhead while improving security posture by facilitating timely renewals.

The ACME protocol operates through challenge-response validation, where a client proves domain control by re- sponding to challenges (such as HTTP-01 or DNS-01). Typical integration involves ACME clients like Certbot, which interact seamlessly with Let's Encrypt to request new certificates, present challenges, and store private keys securely. The automation pipeline involves the following critical steps:

1. Initiate certificate request with ACME client targeting Let's Encrypt

2. Receive domain validation challenge

3. Complete challenge by provisioning the appropriate response in the domain environment

4. Let's Encrypt verifies the challenge response

5. On success, Let's Encrypt issues the certificate

6. ACME client installs the certificate and private key on the server

7. Schedule automatic renewal before certificate expiration

Strict cryptographic policies represent another modern cornerstone. These policies are enforced both on the certificate issuance parameters and the operational TLS stack configuration. Recommended practices include:

- Enforcing minimum key sizes, typically 2048 bits for RSA or employing elliptic curve cryptography such as P-256 or P-384.

- Restricting acceptable signature algorithms to those with robust security profiles, such as ECDSA with SHA-256 or RSA-PSS.

- Mandating certificate transparency submissions to aid in the detection of fraudulent certificates.

- Disallowing deprecated TLS versions (such as TLS 1.0 and 1.1) and cipher suites with known vulnerabilities.

Configuration automation tools often integrate linting and policy compliance checks to ensure all certificates adhere to the organizational security baseline before deployment. These policies not only protect against cryptographic weaknesses but also limit exposure to attacks like downgrade or man-in-the-middle threats.

Automated monitoring forms an essential complement to issuance and renewal processes. By continuously analyzing certificate validity, expiration timeline, and cryptographic compliance, organizations can preempt outages and security incidents. Monitoring solutions utilize a combination of active probes (simulating client connections) and passive telemetry (extracting certificate data from production logs). Alerts are triggered when certificates approach expiration, exhibit anomalies in chain validation, or deviate from specified cryptoprofiles.

Auto-renewal mechanisms rely on scheduled tasks, often implemented as cron jobs or systemd timers, to maintain fresh certificate states without manual intervention. These mechanisms integrate with web servers or load balancers to reload certificate stores seamlessly post-renewal. A typical auto-renewal window initiates the process approximately 30 days prior to expiration, allowing multiple retry attempts in case of transient failures.

Incident handling for certificate failures demands well-defined escalation procedures. Common failure modes include:

- Challenge validation failures, often due to misconfigured DNS records or firewall rules.

- Rate limiting or restrictions imposed by the certificate authority.

- Private key compromise or inappropriate access.

- Certificate revocation or discrepancies in certificate transparency logs.

Response workflows combine automated retries with notification frameworks for human intervention. Incident reports must deliver detailed diagnostic information, including failure type, request metadata, and remediation guidance. In environments with high availability requirements, failover strategies include deploying certificates from secondary authorities or temporarily reverting to previously verified certificates with caution.

An illustrative ACME client configuration snippet demonstrating scheduled auto-renewal with Certbot is provided below:

```
0 3 * * * /usr/bin/certbot renew --quiet --post-hook "
    systemctl reload nginx"
```

This cron job runs daily at 3:00 AM to renew any certificates expiring within 30 days, followed by a reload of the NGINX web server to activate the new certificates without downtime.

Modern TLS certificate management demands a holistic integration of automation protocols such as ACME, rigorous enforcement of cryptographic policies, and proactive operational monitoring. This convergence reduces human error, prevents service disruptions, and upholds cryptographic integrity, forming the foundation for resilient and compliant secure communications.

Chapter 7

Containers and Orchestration

Alpine Linux has set a new standard for minimalism and security in the container revolution, becoming the base image of choice for countless production deployments. This chapter explores the advanced art of building, optimizing, and orchestrating Alpine-powered containers—showing you how to achieve ultra-lightweight footprints, robust security, and seamless scalability. Traverse the full spectrum from image creation to orchestration in Kubernetes and beyond, and learn strategies that the world's best engineering teams rely on for resilience and efficiency.

7.1. Optimizing Alpine for Container Images

Alpine Linux is widely favored for containerized environments due to its minimal footprint and security-oriented design. Leveraging Alpine effectively in production requires a careful approach to image construction that balances size minimization, security hardening, and operational practicality. This section delineates key techniques for crafting Alpine-based container images optimized for production deployment.

Container images are composed of a sequence of layers, each representing changes over the previous state. Efficient image layering reduces the overall image size, promotes cache reuse during builds, and accelerates deployment. When working with Alpine, it is essential to:

- Begin from the official `alpine:latest` base image, which is approximately 5 MB, providing a minimal foundational environment.

- Consolidate package installation commands into a single `RUN` instruction. This prevents unnecessary intermediate layers and eliminates residual package manager caches:

```
FROM alpine:latest
RUN apk add --no-cache bash curl ca-certificates \
    && rm -rf /var/cache/apk/*
```

The --no-cache flag instructs apk to avoid local cache storage, thus obviating the cleanup step. However, including explicit cleanup commands ensures removal of any temporary files created during build.

Minimizing the attack surface is imperative for container security. Alpine's small base aids this objective, but further precautions are necessary:

- Install only strictly necessary packages. Avoid installing packages that bring large dependency trees or provide services unused in production.

166

- Prefer Alpine's `apk` packages over manual installation to benefit from precompiled binaries with security patches.

- Exclude common utilities which might be exploited unless required. For instance, omit shells or scripting languages if the containerized application doesn't depend on them.

- Remove package manager tools and build dependencies after installation in multi-stage builds to prevent proliferation of unnecessary binaries.

A typical strategy is a multi-stage Docker build:

```
# Build stage
FROM alpine:latest AS build
RUN apk add --no-cache build-base
COPY . /src
RUN cd /src && make

# Runtime stage
FROM alpine:latest
COPY --from=build /src/bin/app /usr/local/bin/app
CMD ["app"]
```

This pattern isolates development tools during build and yields a runtime image containing only the essential binary.

A minimal image aligns with faster deployment, reduced attack surface, and lower resource consumption, but overly minimal images may complicate development, troubleshooting, and operations. Delicate compromises can be made:

- Include lightweight shells such as `ash` (provided by Alpine's default `busybox`) for those images where interactive debugging might be necessary.

- Incorporate essential debugging tools (for example,

167

strace, curl, or bash) only in development or staging images, and remove them from production images using multi-stage builds or conditional builds.

- Consider using environment variables or build-time arguments to toggle inclusion of supplementary tools to maintain identical base layers across different environments.

For instance, a flexible build stage may use:

```
ARG INCLUDE_DEBUG=false
RUN if [ "$INCLUDE_DEBUG" = "true" ]; then apk add --no-
    cache bash curl strace; fi
```

This approach enables building either lean production images or richer development images from a common Dockerfile.

While Alpine benefits from a smaller code base by default, further hardening strategies include:

- Enforcing non-root user execution. By default, Alpine containers run as root, which increases risk vectors. Explicitly create and set a non-privileged user for the application process:

```
RUN addgroup -S appgroup && adduser -S appuser -G
    appgroup
USER appuser
```

- Utilizing Alpine's libseccomp and grsecurity-enabled kernel for additional runtime protection. Containers can be started with seccomp profiles to restrict system calls.

- Periodically updating base images and verifying usage of latest security patches in the apk package repository.

- Validating image contents with vulnerability scanners specific for Alpine and container images (for example, `Clair` or `Trivy`).

Optimizing Alpine container images hinges on a
principled trade-off between minimalism, security,
and usability. The adoption of consolidated layer
management, multi-stage builds, selective package
installation, and strict runtime user policies forms a
best practice foundation. The resulting images exhibit
reduced size, hardened attack surfaces, and maintain
operational flexibility necessary for robust production
deployments.

Attention to these practices ensures Alpine continues to excel as a base image choice-combining an ultra-lightweight
footprint with the versatility required in complex containerized infrastructure.

7.2. Docker, Podman, and Alternatives

Container runtimes are fundamental components in modern software development, enabling applications to run in
isolated environments with consistency across diverse systems. Among these, Docker and Podman have emerged as
dominant tools, each offering unique approaches to container lifecycle management, while a range of lightweight
alternatives addresses specialized use cases. When working with Alpine Linux—renowned for its minimalism and
security—understanding these runtimes' interplay with
Linux kernel features such as namespaces and cgroups is
essential for optimal container isolation and performance.

Kernel features underpinning container isolation leverage
several Linux kernel mechanisms to achieve lightweight

yet robust process isolation. The primary components are:

- **Namespaces**: Kernel constructs that isolate global system resources, creating a virtualized environment unique to the processes within the container. Types of namespaces include:

  - *PID namespace*: Isolates process ID number space.
  - *Mount namespace*: Provides an independent filesystem view.
  - *Network namespace*: Segregates networking stack, interfaces, and routing tables.
  - *UTS namespace*: Allows container-specific hostname and domain name.
  - *IPC namespace*: Isolates inter-process communication mechanisms.
  - *User namespace*: Maps container user IDs to host user IDs, enhancing security by running processes as non-root on the host.

- **Control Groups (cgroups)**: Enable resource accounting and limiting, such as CPU shares, memory limits, and I/O bandwidth, ensuring containers do not exceed allocated host resources.

Together, namespaces and cgroups provide a lightweight virtual environment for containers with the efficiency of processes rather than full virtual machines.

Docker, the most widely adopted container runtime, orchestrates the building, distributing, and running of containers. Its architecture consists of the `dockerd` daemon managing container lifecycles and the `docker` CLI client for user interaction. Underneath, Docker uses `runc`, a low-level container runtime compliant with the Open Container Initiative (OCI), to create and start containers by invoking required namespaces and cgroups.

On Alpine Linux, the minimal base image and musl libc reduce image size significantly, making Alpine an ideal minimalistic base for multi-layer Docker images. However, Alpine's busybox and musl environment may require compatibility considerations when running containers designed for systems with GNU libc (glibc).

The process of container initialization with Docker involves:

- Loading an image snapshot.

- Forking a process with isolated namespaces (PID, network, mount, etc.).

- Applying cgroup limits for resource constraints.

- Executing the containerized application as the init process inside the container.

dockerd runs as a root process by default, managing containers system-wide, which simplifies multi-user access but introduces security considerations in multi-tenant environments.

Podman presents an alternative container runtime emphasizing daemonless and rootless operation paradigms. Unlike Docker, Podman does not rely on a central daemon; instead, it spawns containers directly via CLI commands, invoking runc or other OCI-compatible runtimes internally.

Podman's smaller attack surface stems from its daemonless architecture and substantial support for rootless containers. By leveraging user namespaces, Podman maps

171

container user IDs to unprivileged host users, enabling container execution without superuser privileges. This significantly enhances security, making Podman particularly attractive for multi-user systems or environments where privilege escalation risks must be minimized.

Podman is fully compatible with Docker images and most CLI commands, easing migration and adoption on Alpine Linux. Additionally, Podman integrates tightly with systemd, allowing containers to be managed as services, with support for native init systems that are common in Alpine and other minimalist distributions.

Although Docker and Podman dominate, several lightweight container runtimes have gained traction, particularly in scenarios prioritizing minimalism, performance, or specialized needs:

- **Buildah**: Focused primarily on building OCI-compliant images without requiring a daemon. Often paired with Podman for runtime execution.

- **crun**: A lightweight OCI runtime written in C with a smaller memory footprint compared to runc. Optimized for resource-constrained environments such as Alpine-based IoT or embedded systems.

- **Firecracker**: Developed by AWS, Firecracker is a virtualization technology designed for secure, minimal microVMs tailored for serverless computing. It provides isolation via lightweight VMs using KVM, alongside kernel namespaces and cgroups.

- **Kata Containers**: Combine lightweight VMs with container compatibility, providing stronger isolation boundaries at the cost of higher resource use.

These alternatives often excel in environments where minimal overhead, rapid startup times, or enhanced security isolation beyond traditional namespaces and cgroups are required.

Configurability of container runtimes determines the granularity of resource control and isolation mechanisms. Runtime configuration typically involves:

- Specification of user and group IDs within containers to leverage user namespaces and reduce the need for root privileges.

- Mount options to control filesystem visibility and behavior, such as read-only mounts, tmpfs overlays, and bind mounts.

- Network namespace setups ranging from bridged networks to isolated network stacks, configurable through runtime options or orchestration tools.

- Resource limitations via cgroups v1 or v2 interfaces, enabling enforcement of memory caps, CPU quotas, device access controls, and swap usage.

A sample fragment of a minimalist OCI runtime specification for namespace isolation and cgroup limits is as follows:

```
{
  "ociVersion": "1.0.2",
  "process": {
    "user": { "uid": 1000, "gid": 1000 },
    "args": ["sh"],
    "capabilities": null,
    "noNewPrivileges": true
  },
  "linux": {
    "namespaces": [
      { "type": "pid" },
      { "type": "network" },
      { "type": "mount" },
```

```
    { "type": "uts" },
    { "type": "ipc" },
    { "type": "user" }
  ],
  "resources": {
    "memory": { "limit": 536870912 },
    "cpu": { "shares": 512 }
  }
 }
}
```

This configuration initializes a container with comprehensive namespace isolation, a user identity mapped to nonroot, and cgroup-enforced resource limits (512 MiB memory and CPU shares).

Feature	Docker	Podman	Lightweight Alternatives
Daemon Model	Centralized daemon (dockerd)	Daemonless, CLI invokes runtime directly	Varies; often minimal or no daemon
Root Privileges	Requires root or root-equivalent	Supports rootless mode via user namespaces	Varies; often rootless-friendly
Image Compatibility	OCI and Docker images	Fully OCI and Docker compatible	Mostly OCI, focused on performance
Security	Relies on namespace and cgroups, root daemon	Enhanced with rootless, reduced attack surface	Enhanced isolation (microVMs, etc.)
Resource Overhead	Moderate resource overhead due to daemon	Lower overhead without daemon	Minimal overhead, optimized runtime
Ecosystem	Extensive tooling support	Compatible tooling, systemd integration	Specialized use cases, embedded systems

In Alpine environments prioritizing minimalism, Podman offers a compelling balance of security and compatibility without the need for daemon processes. Lightweight runtimes such as crun provide optimized container execution suited to constrained systems. Docker remains the de facto standard for broad compatibility and widespread support, facilitating development workflows that benefit from Alpine's small image size and security posture.

Understanding the underlying container namespace and cgroup architecture remains essential regardless of runtime choice, ensuring correct configuration for isolation, resource allocation, and operational security. This synergy between container runtimes and Alpine's minimalist kernel features enables highly efficient and secure containerized applications.

7.3. Kubernetes and Lightweight Orchestration

Alpine Linux, known for its minimal footprint and security-oriented design, serves as an optimal base for container images, especially when integrated with Kubernetes distributions tailored for lightweight, edge, or resource-constrained environments. Distributions such as k3s, kubeadm, and microk8s leverage Kubernetes' orchestration capabilities while addressing deployment complexity and resource overhead. This section analyzes the deployment and orchestration of Alpine-based containers within these Kubernetes distributions, emphasizing Alpine's role in job scheduling, scaling, and cluster management.

- **k3s**: A certified Kubernetes distribution optimized for resource-constrained devices and edge computing. It consolidates dependencies and uses a single binary under 100MB.

- **kubeadm**: A modular tool providing basic Kubernetes cluster bootstrap without imposing heavy operational abstractions. While not inherently lightweight, it allows tailoring cluster components.

- **microk8s**: A Kubernetes distribution with seamless installation and automatic updates, optimized for local clusters, edge, and IoT devices.

Alpine Linux's compact container images (often under 10MB) complement these distributions by minimizing payload, improving container startup times, and reducing network overhead for image distribution. This synergistic combination is particularly critical for clusters deployed on edge devices, IoT nodes, or virtual machines with limited resources.

Deploying Alpine-based containers on these Kubernetes platforms requires mindful crafting of container manifests and runtime configurations, ensuring Alpine's security and minimalism is preserved without sacrificing Kubernetes' orchestration capabilities:

- **Optimal Image Selection:** Start with Alpine's official images (e.g., `alpine:3.18`) and explicitly manage dependencies to maintain the slim container size, avoiding unnecessary packages.

- **Security Contexts:** Leverage Kubernetes PodSecurityPolicies or Pod Security Admission to restrict container privileges, aligning with Alpine's hardened default settings. Alpine's use of `musl` libc and position-independent executables complement Kubernetes' Seccomp and AppArmor profiles.

- **Resource Requests and Limits:** Set precise CPU and memory limits to capitalize on Alpine's minimal runtime footprint, enabling tighter scheduling on nodes with limited capacity.

```
apiVersion: batch/v1
kind: Job
metadata:
  name: alpine-cleanup
spec:
  template:
    spec:
      containers:
        - name: cleanup-task
          image: alpine:3.18
          command: ["sh", "-c", "rm -rf /tmp/*"]
          resources:
            requests:
              memory: "32Mi"
              cpu: "100m"
            limits:
              memory: "64Mi"
              cpu: "200m"
      restartPolicy: Never
  backoffLimit: 3
```

This manifest exemplifies a resource-conscious job executing a simple cleanup script using an Alpine base image, demonstrating a balance between operational functionality and minimal resource consumption.

Kubernetes offers native abstractions for job scheduling and scaling, which can be enhanced by Alpine-based container strategies:

- **Efficient Job Execution:** Alpine's rapid container startup times (due to smaller images and fewer libraries) reduce pod initialization delays, accelerating job initiation within Kubernetes' batch or CronJob APIs.

- **Horizontal Pod Autoscaling (HPA):** Lightweight images reduce container runtime overhead, affording quicker scale-up responses when CPU or custom metrics thresholds are exceeded.

- **Node Affinity and Taints/Tolerations:** For

edge-centric distributions like k3s or microk8s, Alpine containers can be scheduled preferentially on constrained nodes by defining node affinity rules that match device labels and resource profiles.

Efficient scheduling manifests are crucial when orchestrating workloads with Alpine containers:

```
apiVersion: v1
kind: Pod
metadata:
  name: alpine-edge-worker
spec:
  containers:
  - name: alpine-task
    image: alpine:3.18
    command: ["sh", "-c", "echo Edge processing running;
    sleep 3600"]
    affinity:
      nodeAffinity:
        requiredDuringSchedulingIgnoredDuringExecution:
          nodeSelectorTerms:
          - matchExpressions:
            - key: node.kubernetes.io/edge
              operator: In
              values:
              - "true"
    resources:
      requests:
        memory: "64Mi"
        cpu: "250m"
      limits:
        memory: "128Mi"
        cpu: "500m"
```

This pod manifest schedules Alpine containers explicitly on nodes labeled for edge usage, maximizing cluster resource utilization in heterogeneous environments.

Alpine's characteristics influence cluster management and operational practices:

- **Image Distribution and Caching:** Small Alpine images accelerate deployment workflows across multi-node clusters, especially when network

178

bandwidth is constrained. Kubernetes' image pull policies combined with local registries reduce redundant downloads.

- **Health and Readiness Probes:** Alpine's minimalist shell scripting capability facilitates health checks without additional runtime dependencies, enabling custom probes with simple shell commands in containers.

- **Security Hardened Nodes:** Clusters employing Alpine-based workloads tend to complement hardened node configurations, since Alpine's reduced attack surface aligns with strict pod security and node hardening policies.

Consider a readiness probe example exploiting Alpine's lightweight shell environment:

```
readinessProbe:
  exec:
    command:
    - sh
    - -c
    - test -f /tmp/ready_flag
  initialDelaySeconds: 5
  periodSeconds: 10
```

This probe uses a simple file presence check to determine container readiness, demonstrating the simplicity and flexibility Alpine enables without dependence on external binaries.

While Alpine provides substantial benefits, certain challenges must be addressed:

- **Compatibility with Native Linux Libraries:** Alpine's reliance on musl libc instead of glibc can cause compatibility issues for some software

179

expecting GNU extensions, requiring additional debugging or alternate builds.

- **Debugging and Tooling Limitations:** The minimal nature of Alpine images limits pre-installed debugging tools, necessitating custom image builds including debugging utilities or ephemeral sidecars.

- **Cluster Resource Pressure:** Although Alpine containers minimize resource footprints, cluster operators must carefully size compute and memory allocations to sustain multiple concurrent Alpine workloads at scale.

The combination of Alpine Linux and lightweight Kubernetes distributions such as k3s, kubeadm, and microk8s unlocks efficient, scalable, and secure orchestration paradigms. This enables tailored deployments on resource-constrained clusters, accelerating distributed computing at the cloud edge and embedded systems, where every byte and CPU cycle counts.

7.4. Security in the Container Stack

Containerization introduces a paradigm shift in workload deployment, enabling rapid scaling and efficient resource utilization. However, the abstraction it provides also expands the attack surface, demanding advanced security mechanisms to protect containerized applications. This section explores critical security features of the container stack, including Linux capabilities, seccomp filtering, AppArmor/SELinux integration, the management of Common Vulnerabilities and Exposures (CVEs), and effective hardening and compliance strategies for production environments.

Linux Capabilities: Fine-Grained Privilege Control

The traditional Unix permission model, rooted in the all-or-nothing root/non-root distinction, is insufficient for securing container workloads. Linux capabilities enable granular privilege partitioning by decomposing the root user's privileges into discrete units. Containers typically run as root inside their namespace, posing significant risk if those privileges map directly to host privileges.

Capabilities in containers are managed via the cap_drop and cap_add configuration options of container runtimes. By default, most runtimes employ a baseline capability set to minimize exposure. For example, capabilities like CAP_SYS_ADMIN, which grants nearly unrestricted kernel access, should always be dropped unless explicitly required. Essential capabilities such as CAP_NET_BIND_SERVICE (allowing binding to ports below 1024) or CAP_CHOWN may be selectively retained per workload requirements.

```
# Example Docker run command dropping all capabilities
    except NET_BIND_SERVICE
docker run --cap-drop=ALL --cap-add=NET_BIND_SERVICE
    mycontainer
```

Employing capabilities judiciously reduces the risk of privilege escalation attacks within containers, enforcing a principle of least privilege.

seccomp: System Call Filtering for Attack Surface Reduction

Containers share the host kernel, making system calls a critical control point. seccomp (secure computing mode) enables the filtering of system calls available to a container process, significantly narrowing the kernel interface exposed to potentially vulnerable user-space applications.

Container runtimes support seccomp profiles, often specified in JSON format, to whitelist or blacklist system calls. The default Docker seccomp profile denies uncommon or dangerous calls such as `keyctl` or `acct` that are rarely needed for typical workloads but have been exploited historically.

```
{
  "syscalls": [
    {
      "names": ["clone"],
      "action": "SCMP_ACT_ERRNO",
      "args": [
        {
          "index": 0,
          "value": 0x10000000,
          "op": "SCMP_CMP_MASKED_EQ"
        }
      ]
    }
  ]
}
```

This example denies any `clone` calls attempting to create new user namespaces, a common vector in privilege escalation exploits when running containers with elevated permissions.

AppArmor and SELinux: Mandatory Access Control Enforcement

Mandatory Access Control (MAC) frameworks encode security policies that constrain container processes beyond traditional discretionary access control (DAC) models. Both AppArmor and SELinux integrate tightly with container runtimes to enforce access restrictions on file systems, process capabilities, and IPC resources.

AppArmor profiles, designed with a path-based approach, specify allowed file permissions and system operations for containerized processes. Kubernetes and Docker enable AppArmor through annotations and runtime labels, allowing fine-grained confinement for containers. Unconfined containers lack these protections and should be avoided in production.

SELinux operates based on a labeling system that classifies containers and resources with types, enforcing policy rules on how those types interact. For example, the default SELinux context prevents containers from accessing host resources arbitrarily. Administrators can customize module policies to accommodate application-specific access needs while preserving containment.

The interplay between these MAC systems and container runtimes helps prevent lateral movement, privilege escalation, and unauthorized resource access even if a container is compromised.

CVE Management: Continuous Vulnerability Monitoring and Patching

Containers rely heavily on underlying base images and open source dependencies, both of which may contain known vulnerabilities cataloged as CVEs. An effective security posture mandates continuous scanning for known CVEs throughout the build and deployment lifecycle.

Static and dynamic image scanning tools such as Clair, Trivy, and Anchore integrate into CI/CD pipelines to identify vulnerable packages, outdated libraries, or misconfigurations before images are deployed. Once vulnerabilities are detected, base images should be updated promptly to patched versions, and dependent applications must be rebuilt to incorporate fixes.

A rigorous CVE management workflow involves:

- Automated vulnerability scanning at build time and runtime.

183

- Prioritization based on CVSS scores and exploitability.

- Timely base image updates and rebuilds.

- Use of minimal base images (e.g., distroless or scratch) to reduce attack surface.

Compliance with industry standards, such as PCI DSS or HIPAA, often prescribes documented vulnerability management cycles and proof of remediation.

Hardening and Compliance Strategies

Beyond individual security controls, a holistic hardening strategy encompasses layered defense, adherence to best practices, and continuous monitoring:

- **Run as Non-root User**: Containers should execute with minimal privileges. Where root is necessary inside a container namespace, ensure host namespace mappings prevent escalation.

- **Immutable Container Filesystems**: Using read-only filesystems limits unauthorized modifications.

- **Network Policies**: Employ network segmentation and fine-grained ingress/egress controls using tools like Kubernetes Network Policies or Cilium to limit attack propagation.

- **Secrets Management**: Avoid embedding secrets in images or environment variables; use external secret stores with strict access controls.

- **Audit Logging and Runtime Security**: Collect container logs and runtime telemetry to detect anomalies and enforce policy compliance using tools like Falco or Sysdig Secure.

- **Supply Chain Security**: Validate the provenance of images, sign artifacts, and use trusted registries.

Operational frameworks such as the CIS Docker Benchmark and NIST guidelines provide prescriptive checklists to measure security posture. Organizations can integrate these benchmarks as Gatekeeper policies in Kubernetes or automate assessments with compliance scanning tools to ensure ongoing adherence.

Together, Linux kernel capabilities, seccomp syscall filtering, robust MAC policies via AppArmor and SELinux, and rigorous CVE management, implemented within a defense-in-depth architecture, establish a resilient security foundation for container workloads. This multi-faceted approach minimizes the risk of container breakout, lateral movement, and supply chain compromise, vital to maintaining trustworthy container deployments at scale.

7.5. Container Networking, Storage, and Logging

Containerized applications mandate precise orchestration of networking, storage, and logging subsystems to ensure robust functionality, data persistence, and observability. These infrastructure elements are pivotal for complex microservices architectures and stateful applications, and their configuration directly impacts performance, reliability, and operational insights.

Multi-Networking Configuration

By default, containers are connected to a single virtual network bridge, often limiting traffic segmentation and security controls. Multi-networking enables containers to interface with multiple networks simultaneously, providing logical separation and distinct routing paths without deploying additional hosts.

Containers leverage network namespaces to isolate interfaces and routing tables. To configure multi-networking, container runtime tools such as Docker or container orchestration platforms like Kubernetes rely on Container Network Interface (CNI) plugins. Each CNI plugin facilitates dynamic attachment of container interfaces to one or more networks defined at runtime or via configuration files.

A typical Kubernetes pod can be connected to several networks utilizing Multus CNI, which acts as a meta-plugin allowing multiple network attachments. Configuration involves declaring secondary networks in CustomResourceDefinitions and modifying pod annotations to specify network attachments:

```
apiVersion: k8s.cni.cncf.io/v1
kind: NetworkAttachmentDefinition
metadata:
  name: secondary-net
spec:
  config: '{
    "cniVersion": "0.3.1",
    "type": "macvlan",
    "mode": "bridge",
    "master": "eth0",
    "ipam": {
      "type": "static",
      "addresses": [
        {
          "address": "192.168.1.100/24",
          "gateway": "192.168.1.1"
        }
      ]
    }
  }'
```

Container pods annotated to attach to this network receive an additional interface with its own IP address, enabling traffic segregation:

```
metadata:
  annotations:
    k8s.v1.cni.cncf.io/networks: secondary-net
```

Common challenges include IP address management and ensuring network policy enforcement across multiple interfaces. Adopting centralized IP Address Management (IPAM) and leveraging Kubernetes Network Policies for each network interface mitigates these challenges, preserving security boundaries and traffic flow control.

Persistent Storage Volumes

Ephemeral containers necessitate persistent storage volumes to maintain state beyond container lifetimes. Container runtimes abstract storage through volume mounting strategies, enabling data to survive container restarts and rescheduling.

In Docker, declaring volumes involves explicit specification in the container creation command or Docker Compose files:

```
volumes:
  - type: volume
    source: my_data_volume
    target: /var/lib/data
```

Kubernetes offers a sophisticated persistent volume (PV) and persistent volume claim (PVC) abstraction to provision, claim, and bind storage dynamically from underlying infrastructure such as Network File System (NFS), cloud block storage, or distributed storage systems like Ceph and GlusterFS.

A standard PVC example dynamically allocates a persistent volume:

```
apiVersion: v1
kind: PersistentVolumeClaim
```

```
metadata:
  name: data-pvc
spec:
  accessModes:
    - ReadWriteOnce
  resources:
    requests:
      storage: 10Gi
```

The pod references the PVC to mount the associated volume:

```
spec:
  containers:
  - name: app
    image: example/app
    volumeMounts:
    - mountPath: /data
      name: data-volume
  volumes:
  - name: data-volume
    persistentVolumeClaim:
      claimName: data-pvc
```

Persistent storage presents challenges such as ensuring consistent data access, volume reclaim policies, and performance tuning. Employing ReadWriteMany volumes can enable shared access across multiple pods, balancing consistency and concurrency. Furthermore, Storage-Classes with appropriate reclaim policies (e.g., Retain, Delete) allow controlled lifecycle management of volumes and underlying storage.

Avoiding data corruption requires careful control of volume access modes in clustered file systems and awareness of filesystem compatibility with container images.

Efficient Log Stream Integration

Container log management plays a critical role in observability by aggregating, filtering, and forwarding logs in real-time. Containers emit logs primarily through standard output and error streams, captured at the container runtime level. However, the ephemeral nature of containers demands centralized log aggregation to avoid loss and to facilitate analysis.

Log collection agents such as Fluentd, Logstash, or dedicated Kubernetes DaemonSets (e.g., Fluent Bit) tail container log files and forward them to centralized systems like Elasticsearch, Kafka, or cloud log services. The configuration for efficient logging should incorporate structured logging formats (e.g., JSON) to enable efficient parsing and filtering downstream.

A common pattern in Kubernetes clusters involves sidecar containers dedicated to log shipping, isolating logging responsibilities and reducing application container complexity:

```
apiVersion: v1
kind: Pod
metadata:
  name: log-example
spec:
  containers:
  - name: app
    image: example/app
  - name: log-agent
    image: fluent/fluent-bit
    volumeMounts:
    - name: varlog
      mountPath: /var/log/containers
  volumes:
  - name: varlog
    hostPath:
      path: /var/log/containers
```

Critical considerations include controlling log verbosity to prevent storage exhaustion and implementing retention policies at log ingestion systems. Persistent storage backing log collections enables historical auditing and troubleshooting.

Observability tools integrate with logging systems to correlate logs with metrics and traces, providing comprehensive insight into container behavior. Service meshes and instrumentation frameworks further enhance log context by injecting metadata and tracing identifiers.

Common obstacles are log volume spikes during failures or verbose debug modes and log format inconsistencies across microservices. Employing rate limiting, sampling, and enforcing logging standards mitigates these issues.

Overcoming Data Retention and Observability Challenges

Effective container deployments confront two primary operational challenges: retaining data reliably and maintaining actionable observability without resource overhead.

For persistence, implementing tiered storage solutions combining fast ephemeral caches with durable volume backends balances performance with reliability. Backups and snapshots must integrate seamlessly with volume APIs to create consistent recovery points.

In observability, adopting hierarchical logging architectures reduces noise by aggregating logs at multiple levels before forwarding. Correlating logs with contextual metadata from orchestration platforms ensures precise filtering and analysis.

Service-level log rotation and retention policies reduce disk consumption on nodes. Centralized retention policies must comply with regulatory requirements while enabling forensic investigations.

Automated instrumentation and monitoring pipelines utilizing agents and collectors ensure continuous observability, offering proactive alerting on anomalous events linked to networking disruptions, storage failures, or logging pipeline errors.

The confluence of multi-networking, persistent storage, and efficient logging within containerized environments forms the backbone of resilient and transparent systems. Mastery of configuration and mitigation strategies in these domains directly enhances the operational excellence and scalability of container deployments.

7.6. Building and Publishing Custom Images

Automation of multi-architecture builds has become a foundational requirement in modern containerized environments to ensure broad deployment compatibility and operational consistency. The process begins with defining build pipelines that target multiple hardware architectures, commonly amd64, arm64, and occasionally ppc64le or s390x. Tools such as Docker Buildx enable this capability by leveraging QEMU emulation and remote build contexts to orchestrate cross-platform image builds within a single workflow. A typical multi-architecture build pipeline involves creating platform-specific manifests and consolidating these manifests into a unified image index, often referred to as a manifest list, which clients can pull transparently based on the target architecture.

The cryptographic signing of container images is imperative for trust assurance and tamper evidence. Technologies like Notary v2 and Sigstore have established frameworks for signing and verification workflows. These systems employ public key infrastructures (PKI) or transparency logs to enable image authors and consumers to verify image provenance and integrity reliably. The signing process involves generating cryptographic signatures on image digests rather than the image layers themselves, ensuring immutability and consistency as layers traverse registries. Integration with automated build pipelines further ensures that signing is a mandated step before images move forward in deployment workflows, preventing unsigned or unverified artifacts from reaching production environments.

Promotion workflows amplify security by managing staged progression of container images through development, testing, staging, and production environments. This is realized using registry tag immutability alongside declarative policies in ramp-up tools. For instance, after an image passes a battery of automated tests in the development environment, it receives a signed promotion tag such as `promoted-dev-to-staging`. This tag triggers downstream pipelines that pull the exact, immutable image digest, run additional integration and security tests, and upon success, apply a `promoted-staging-to-prod` signature. Such workflows minimize human error and enforce strict immutability guarantees-images once promoted are never altered or overridden, facilitating reliable rollback and audit criteria.

Publishing custom images requires adherence to best practices that promote usability, security, and maintainability. Clear semantic versioning combined with human-readable tags simplifies consumption and debugging in operational contexts. Image metadata labels compliant with the OCI Image Format Specification enhance metadata discoverability for automated tools and improve traceability. Best practices also dictate minimizing image sizes by selecting appropriate base images and employing multi-stage builds that discard build-time dependencies, thus reducing attack surfaces and improving runtime efficiency. Moreover, publishing endpoints must support secure transport (TLS) and authentication protocols such as OAuth or Basic Auth to ensure confidentiality and prevent unauthorized modification or download.

Integration of multi-architecture build and publishing workflows into Continuous Integration and Continuous Deployment (CI/CD) pipelines is critical for operational agility. Modern CI/CD tools such as Jenkins, GitLab CI, GitHub Actions, and Tekton offer native or plugin-based support for container image builds, signing, promotion, and deployment. Pipelines are typically defined as code, using YAML or domain-specific languages, embedding steps for multi-arch builds via Buildx or Kaniko, followed by cryptographic signing steps using tools like Cosign. Promotion logic is encoded as conditional stages, ensuring controlled gatekeeping based on test outcomes or manual approvals. For example:

```
stages:
  - build
  - sign
  - promote

build:
  image: docker
  script:
    - docker buildx create --use
    - docker buildx build --platform linux/amd64,linux/
      arm64 --push -t registry.example.com/myimage:${
      CI_COMMIT_SHA} .
sign:
  image: sigstore/cosign
  script:
    - cosign sign --key cosign.key registry.example.com/
      myimage:${CI_COMMIT_SHA}
promote:
  when: manual
  script:
    - docker pull registry.example.com/myimage:${
      CI_COMMIT_SHA}
    - docker tag registry.example.com/myimage:${
      CI_COMMIT_SHA} registry.example.com/myimage:stable
    - docker push registry.example.com/myimage:stable
```

Enforcing immutable tags and digest pinning within deployment manifests, for example, Kubernetes manifests, ensures that exact image versions are deployed across environments without drift. Policies implemented within CI/CD pipelines can additionally incorporate vulnerability scanning results, digital signature verification, and compliance checks before promotion or deployment stages proceed.

The synergy of automated multi-architecture builds, cryptographic signing, and secure promotion workflows establishes a robust foundation for delivering trustworthy and portable container images. When combined with best practices in publishing and seamless CI/CD integration, these capabilities provide software engineering teams with scalable and secure mechanisms to manage containerized applications from initial development to production release.

Chapter 8

Advanced Security and Hardening Techniques

Security isn't achieved by chance—it's engineered with intent. Alpine Linux empowers you to build systems where minimalism and security are tightly interwoven, enabling formidable defense layers unknown to bulkier distributions. This chapter uncovers the strategies, kernel features, and automation frameworks that make Alpine a premier choice for hardened, resilient environments. Go beyond the basics and learn to orchestrate proactive security, compliance, and rapid response—meeting the ever-evolving threat landscape with confidence.

8.1. Kernel Hardening and Minimalism

The kernel serves as the critical foundation of any operating system, mediating resource access and enforcing security policies. While upstream Linux kernels provide a baseline level of security, enhancing resilience in hostile environments necessitates deliberate hardening and minimization tailored to Alpine Linux's principles of simplicity and security. This section explores the strategies used to customize and fortify the Alpine kernel, focusing on hardened profiles, the integration of `grsecurity` and `PaX`, as well as Alpine-specific patches, culminating in techniques aimed at shrinking the kernel attack surface and constructing security-optimized custom kernels.

Hardened Profiles: Principles and Implementation

Hardened profiles constitute a set of kernel and system-wide configuration parameters designed to enforce stricter security boundaries beyond default configurations. Alpine Linux leverages the `hardened` configuration flags, which extend compiler and kernel options to minimize common vulnerabilities such as buffer overflows, use-after-free errors, and privilege escalations.

Key kernel configuration options within hardened profiles include:

- `CONFIG_STRICT_DEVMEM`: Restricts kernel memory access through `/dev/mem` to prevent hardware-level exploits.

- `CONFIG_DEBUG_RODATA`: Marks kernel read-only data as non-executable, mitigating code injection attempts.

196

- `CONFIG_STACKPROTECTOR_STRONG`: Enables compiler-level stack overflow protection.

- `CONFIG_KERNEL_KASLR`: Activates Kernel Address Space Layout Randomization to hinder certain types of memory exploits.

Within Alpine, the hardened profile is encapsulated in the `linux-hardened` kernel flavor, which integrates these options with Alpine-specific packaging policies ensuring compatibility and stability without compromising security hardening.

Integration of Grsecurity and PaX

`grsecurity` represents a prominent kernel patchset designed to improve security by a combination of exploit mitigations, access control enhancements, and auditing capabilities. Though not included in mainline Linux due to its restrictive licensing and maintenance model, Alpine accommodates `grsecurity` in dedicated packages and custom builds to satisfy high-security use cases.

The `PaX` patch, bundled within `grsecurity`, provides advanced memory protection techniques, including:

- **Non-executable Memory Regions**: Ensures pages designated for data cannot be executed, preventing common buffer overflow exploits.

- **Address Space Layout Randomization (ASLR)**: Randomizes the location of executable code in process memory space.

- **Memory Protections such as `MPROTECT` Restrictions**: Limits the ability to change memory page permissions at runtime.

Applying grsecurity and PaX patches to Alpine kernels involves patching the kernel source tree prior to package compilation. Alpine's build infrastructure supports these automated patch applications, maintaining consistency across kernel versions. The resulting kernel enforces stringent memory safety and elevates kernel internals' integrity, at the potential cost of some performance overhead and increased kernel size.

Alpine-Specific Kernel Patches

Beyond upstream hardening and grsecurity, Alpine introduces its own set of kernel patches tailored for minimalism and security. These patches prune or disable rarely used kernel functionality to reduce the attack surface and enhance auditability. Examples include:

- **Disabling Obsolete Network Protocols**: Legacy services such as IPX, AppleTalk, and DECnet are removed or disabled unless explicitly required.

- **Module Blacklisting and Simplification**: Unneeded kernel modules identified through usage statistics or threat modeling are either blacklisted or removed from builds.

- **System Call Filtering**: Alpine enables additional system call filtering mechanisms at the kernel level to prevent abuse of rarely used or insecure syscalls.

These patches contribute to kernel minimalism by removing code paths that could harbor vulnerabilities, thus simplifying kernel auditing and reducing maintenance complexity.

Attack Surface Reduction Techniques

A primary goal of kernel hardening is the reduction of the kernel's attack surface: the aggregate of code and interfaces exposed to potential exploitation. Techniques can be grouped into static and dynamic approaches:

Static Reduction focuses on kernel selection and configuration prior to compilation. Alpine utilizes tailored kernel defconfig files to exclude non-essential features and drivers, minimize kernel modules, and configure stricter defaults. Moreover, techniques such as enabling kernel optional entropy checks, enhancing permission constraints on debug interfaces, and disabling legacy compatibility layers harden the baseline kernel.

Dynamic Reduction involves runtime controls and monitoring to guard kernel integrity. Control groups (cgroups) can limit resource usage, while Linux Security Modules (LSMs) such as AppArmor or SELinux work in conjunction with hardened kernel capabilities to enforce granular access policies. Additionally, kernel lockdown modes restrict kernel access via interfaces like /dev/mem or kernel module loading once the system is in a restricted state.

Building Security-Optimized Custom Kernels

The creation of custom Alpine kernels optimized for security demands a structured approach combining hardening features, patches, and minimization strategies:

- Define security requirements by establishing threat models specific to the deployment environment, prioritizing required protections versus usability or performance.

- Select kernel flavor and patchsets, choosing between Alpine's linux-hardened, grsecurity-patched kernels, or a vanilla kernel with selected patches.

- Apply minimal configurations using Alpine-specific kernel configuration profiles emphasizing minimalism, stripping non-essential drivers and features.

- Integrate Alpine-specific patches by applying Alpine's curated security patches that reduce attack vectors without compromising compatibility.

- Compile with hardened toolchains using GCC Hardened toolchain options such as `-fstack-protector-strong`, `-D_FORTIFY_SOURCE=2`, and others to enhance binary security.

- Test and audit by performing comprehensive functionality and security testing using kernel audit subsystems, syscall tracing, and fuzzing tools to verify hardening effectiveness.

An example `make` command for building a hardened Alpine kernel with `grsecurity` patches might be:

```
export KERNEL_PATCHVER=5.15
export GRSECURITY_VERSION=4.15-2023091200
cd /usr/src/linux-${KERNEL_PATCHVER}
patch -p1 < /usr/src/grsecurity-${GRSECURITY_VERSION}.
    patch
make alpine_defconfig
make -j$(nproc) LOCALVERSION=-grsec
```

```
Kernel: 5.15.45-grsec
Features enabled: PaX, KASLR, Stack Protector, Strict DEVMEM
Modules: minimal set according to configuration
Size on disk: 12 MB (compressed)
Boot time overhead: approx. +5%
```

Trade-offs and Considerations

Kernel hardening and minimalism entail trade-offs between increased security, performance, and functionality. Aggressive patching and minimization can result in incompatibilities with kernel modules or third-party drivers. Additionally, overhead from mitigations like `grsecurity/PaX` or KASLR may affect system responsiveness, necessitating profiling and tuning based on use-case constraints.

Moreover, maintaining custom hardened kernels requires continuous updates aligned with upstream security patches. Alpine's infrastructure eases this burden by integrating hardened kernels into its build and packaging systems, but operators must still maintain vigilance against kernel-level vulnerabilities.

Ultimately, the combination of hardened profiles, `grsecurity` integration, Alpine-specific security patches, and attack surface reduction techniques forms a robust framework for building secure, minimal, and resilient kernels suitable for containment-focused or threat-sensitive environments.

8.2. Mandatory Access Control: AppArmor and Alternatives

Mandatory Access Control (MAC) mechanisms enforce system security by imposing strict and non-bypassable policies on subjects and objects, independent of user discretion. Unlike discretionary controls, MAC confines processes to explicitly defined privileges, significantly reducing the risk surface for privilege escalation and unauthorized access. AppArmor stands out among Linux implementations of MAC due to its path-based approach, ease of integration, and granular policy definition. This section examines AppArmor in depth, its policy structure, profile writing, tuning mechanisms, and contrasts it with prominent alternatives such as SELinux and TOMOYO Linux.

AppArmor enforces security by associating executable programs with profiles that specify permitted file operations, network access, and capability usage. Each profile constrains a program's execution context, restricting it to a subset of system resources as defined by policy writers. Profiles rely on filesystem pathnames rather than labels, which simplifies policy comprehension and management in many scenarios but requires careful maintenance to avoid path ambiguities.

Profile Structure and Syntax

An AppArmor profile comprises rules arranged hierarchically, each granting or denying access to specific resources. Profiles begin with the program executable's absolute path, followed by an optional profile mode declaration:

```
/usr/bin/example-profile {
    # Mode flags: complain, enforce, or unconfined
    # Rules are specified here
}
```

Two principal rule types govern file access: path rules and capability rules. Path rules enumerate filesystem paths alongside access modes—read (r), write (w), execute (x), and link (l). The following example restricts a process to reading specific configuration files and executing binaries within /usr/bin:

```
/etc/example.conf r,
/usr/bin/** px,
```

The wildcard ** matches directories recursively. Capability rules limit process privileges beyond file access, controlling kernel capabilities such as net_bind_service, dac_override, or setuid. Explicit denial of sensitive capabilities curtails privilege escalation vectors. For instance:

```
capability net_bind_service,
deny capability setuid,
```

AppArmor also supports abstractions and includes to reuse common policy snippets, easing profile maintenance and promoting modularity. Abstractions define sets of permissions for typical actions or subsystems, which can be included using the @ syntax:

```
@include <abstractions/base>
@include <abstractions/nameservice>
```

Policy Writing and Tuning

Constructing effective AppArmor profiles involves a cycle of initial confinement, monitoring, and refinement. The process starts by generating a permissive profile using system audit logs or AppArmor's learning mode (complain), which logs access violations without blocking. The aa-genprof tool facilitates interactive profile creation:

```
sudo aa-genprof /usr/bin/example
```

This utility guides the administrator through notifications of accesses, enabling granular permission additions. The profile is iteratively hardened by switching to enforcement mode (enforce) once the policy sufficiently supports legitimate operation without denials.

Effective tuning demands close monitoring via AppArmor's logging subsystem, typically accessible through the kernel's audit system or utilities such as dmesg. Logged violations under enforced profiles correspond to attempted policy violations and provide actionable feedback for necessary rule adjustments:

```
type=APPARMOR_MSG msg=audit(1618321234.123:567): profile="example"
operation="open" name="/etc/secret.conf" pid=1234 comm="example" requested_ma
sk="r" denied_mask="r"
```

Addressing such denials may involve adding exception rules cautiously, ensuring that broad permissions are not granted inadvertently, preserving the principle of least privilege.

Integration and System-Wide Enforcement

AppArmor integrates into the Linux Security Modules (LSM) framework and is often enabled by default in several distributions such as Ubuntu and SUSE. Profiles can be loaded and reloaded dynamically without rebooting, enabling responsive security management. The management suite offers commands including aa-status, aa-enforce, and aa-disable to query and manipulate profile states:

```
sudo aa-status
sudo aa-enforce /usr/bin/example
sudo aa-disable /usr/bin/example
```

System administrators are encouraged to profile all critical system services and network-facing daemons, confining them to minimal functionalities required for operation. AppArmor's clarity and path-based semantics facilitate integration with containerized environments and automated deployment pipelines where reproducibility and auditability are paramount.

Alternatives: SELinux and TOMOYO Linux

SELinux represents another widely deployed MAC implementation, distinguished by its label-based Mandatory Access Control. SELinux policies operate on the principle of assigning security contexts to all system objects, which promotes fine-grained control and comprehensive confinement but entails a steeper learning curve and increased configuration complexity.

SELinux policy syntax employs types and roles, with finely

articulated rules in type enforcement (TE) files. It generally provides more extensive control over interprocess communication and system resources than AppArmor, albeit at the cost of greater administrative overhead.

TOMOYO Linux offers path-based MAC similar to AppArmor but extends policy generation capabilities through automatic observation of process behavior during normal operation. It constructs granular rulesets based on actual execution traces, facilitating rapid bootstrap of policies that can later be audited and refined.

Comparison of the three indicates that AppArmor's simplicity suits environments where ease of deployment and maintainability outweigh the need for deep, granular controls. SELinux is appropriate in high-assurance environments where strict system behavior enforcement is crucial, while TOMOYO's adaptive policy building appeals to use cases requiring dynamic, behavior-driven profiling.

Preventing Privilege Escalation with MAC Policies

By limiting processes to minimal filesystem access, network operations, and capabilities, AppArmor effectively mitigates classic vectors for privilege escalation attacks, such as unauthorized invocation of setuid binaries, arbitrary file modifications, or network service binding. Capability drops are particularly instrumental in constraining processes from gaining elevated system control, for example banning `cap_sys_admin` or `cap_setuid`.

Furthermore, profile confinement can isolate vulnerable services within sandboxes, confining damage from potential exploitation to specifically authorized resources. Combined with kernel seccomp filters and namespaces, MAC policies establish layered defenses within the principle of defense-in-depth.

The explicit denial of undesired actions creates a default-deny posture, where processes are allowed only explicitly granted operations. AppArmor's granular controls enable this posture while maintaining operational transparency through `complain` mode, which is crucial during policy development.

Summary of Best Practices

- Begin with permissive `complain` mode profiles and iteratively refine rules through audit log analysis.

- Restrict filesystem access using path-based rules, limiting wildcard usage where possible to minimize unintended access.

- Restrict capabilities to the minimal required set; deny all others explicitly.

- Use abstraction includes and modular profile components for maintainability.

- Enforce policies on all exposed network services and critical system processes.

- Employ automated tools (`aa-genprof`, `aa-logprof`) to assist in profile generation and tuning.

- Continuously monitor audit logs for policy violations and update the profiles accordingly.

In sum, AppArmor and equivalent MAC mechanisms provide indispensable tools for enforcing the principle of least privilege through mandatory controls. Their correct deployment significantly hardens systems against privilege escalation and unauthorized access, constituting essential components of a modern Linux security architecture.

8.3. Filesystem Security and Encryption

Full disk encryption (FDE) serves as a fundamental defense layer to protect data at rest, ensuring that all stored information is rendered inaccessible without proper authorization. Modern Linux systems extensively utilize two prominent technologies for this purpose: LUKS (Linux Unified Key Setup) and eCryptfs (Enterprise Cryptographic Filesystem). Each offers distinct advantages and operational models for securing sensitive data, complementing file integrity monitoring tools designed to detect unauthorized modifications during both live operation and offline analysis.

LUKS operates at the block device layer, providing transparent encryption for entire disk partitions before the filesystem layer is mounted. By encrypting the raw block device, it guarantees that all data, including metadata and filesystem structures, are secured. LUKS uses DM-Crypt as its backend, integrating encryption within the device-mapper framework. The cryptographic key management infrastructure supports multiple key slots, enabling separate passwords or keys to unlock the encrypted volume without compromising the underlying master key. This facilitates flexible recovery and access control policies.

A typical LUKS workflow begins with partition preparation, where cryptsetup initializes the encrypted volume:

```
cryptsetup luksFormat /dev/sdXn
cryptsetup luksOpen /dev/sdXn encrypted_volume
mkfs.ext4 /dev/mapper/encrypted_volume
mount /dev/mapper/encrypted_volume /secure/data
```

Once the encrypted volume is unlocked and mounted, all I/O operations are automatically encrypted and decrypted by the device-mapper layer. This method greatly simplifies user interaction, requiring no changes to the applications that read or write data, while providing strong cryptographic guarantees.

In contrast, eCryptfs functions at the filesystem layer, operating as a stacked cryptographic filesystem that encrypts individual files rather than entire partitions. This enables targeted protection of specific directories or user home spaces, often integrated with per-user keys. eCryptfs is particularly useful when encryption granularities or cross-platform portability are needed, since encrypted files remain accessible on other systems supporting eCryptfs, provided the keys are available.

Installation and mounting of an eCryptfs encrypted directory typically proceed as follows:

```
mount -t ecryptfs /home/user/.Private /home/user/Private
```

During this mount operation, options specify encryption algorithms (e.g., AES), key signatures, and passphrases. Files stored within the mounted directory are encrypted individually using the specified keys, allowing fine-tuned access control. However, unlike LUKS, metadata such as filenames or directory structures may reveal limited information unless filename encryption is enabled.

Beyond encryption, maintaining filesystem integrity is critical to detecting and responding to unauthorized modifications or tampering. File integrity monitoring (FIM) tools play a key role in this regard by establishing trusted baselines of file hashes and attributes against which subsequent checks validate system state. Tools such as Tripwire, AIDE (Advanced Intrusion Detection Environment), and Samhain enable automated detection of suspicious changes, signaling potential compromises or accidental corruption.

The operation of FIM tools involves two primary phases:

initial baseline creation and periodic verification. The baseline is generated by recursively hashing target directories with cryptographic hash functions such as SHA-256, recording metadata like file size, permissions, and modification timestamps. The subsequent verification scans compare current states against this baseline, highlighting discrepancies.

For example, the AIDE initialization and check commands are as follows:

```
aide --init
mv /var/lib/aide/aide.db.new /var/lib/aide/aide.db
aide --check
```

Outputs list files modified, added, or removed since the baseline, assisting system administrators in focusing investigation efforts. When integrated with system logging and alerting frameworks, these tools provide timely detection of evolving threats.

The combination of robust full disk encryption and vigilant file integrity verification delivers a comprehensive framework for protecting sensitive data in both live and dormant states. LUKS ensures that data at rest is cryptographically inaccessible without appropriate credentials, thwarting offline physical attacks. eCryptfs enhances protection through targeted encryption at the file level, suitable for multi-user environments and scenarios requiring flexibility. Meanwhile, integrity monitoring detects subtle and potentially malicious filesystem changes that encryption alone cannot prevent, forming an indispensable part of a layered defense strategy.

Deploying these technologies collectively requires careful key management policies, secure initialization procedures, and regular integrity audits tailored to organizational threat models. Ensuring passphrase complexity, implementing hardware root-of-trust mechanisms such as TPMs, and integrating with automated alerting frameworks can further reinforce these protections.

Safeguarding filesystem data demands a dual emphasis on cryptographic confidentiality and integrity assurance. Leveraging LUKS and eCryptfs addresses the protection of data at rest, while systematic deployment of file integrity monitoring tools enables proactive detection of unauthorized changes in live environments. This synergy forms the foundation for resilient filesystem security in modern Linux infrastructures.

8.4. System Resource Sandboxing

System resource sandboxing is a fundamental technique for enforcing isolation and resource control on processes, particularly when dealing with untrusted or potentially compromised code. By combining Linux kernel primitives—seccomp, namespaces, and cgroups—an effective sandbox can be constructed that limits the capabilities, visibility, and resource consumption of contained processes. This section elaborates on the setup and management of such sandboxed environments, emphasizing their role in security and system stability.

Seccomp: System Call Filtering

Seccomp (secure computing mode) provides a mechanism to restrict the system calls a process can invoke, thereby reducing the attack surface exposed by the kernel interface. There are two primary modes in seccomp:

- **Strict mode**: Allows only four system calls (read, write, _exit, sigreturn).

- **Filter mode**: Allows selective filtering based on detailed rules using Berkeley Packet Filter (BPF) programs.

Filter mode is most applicable for sophisticated sandboxes, implemented via the `seccomp()` system call with `SECCOMP_SET_MODE_FILTER` and a BPF program defining allowed system call numbers and conditions. For example, a minimal filter that only allows file descriptor operations can be coded as:

```
#include <linux/seccomp.h>
#include <linux/filter.h>
#include <linux/audit.h>
#include <sys/prctl.h>
#include <seccomp.h>

int install_seccomp_filter() {
    scmp_filter_ctx ctx;

    ctx = seccomp_init(SCMP_ACT_KILL); // Default action
     : kill
    if (!ctx) return -1;

    // Allow essential syscalls
    seccomp_rule_add(ctx, SCMP_ACT_ALLOW, SCMP_SYS(read)
     , 0);
    seccomp_rule_add(ctx, SCMP_ACT_ALLOW, SCMP_SYS(write
     ), 0);
    seccomp_rule_add(ctx, SCMP_ACT_ALLOW, SCMP_SYS(exit)
     , 0);
    seccomp_rule_add(ctx, SCMP_ACT_ALLOW, SCMP_SYS(
     exit_group), 0);

    int rc = seccomp_load(ctx);
    seccomp_release(ctx);
    return rc;
}
```

Upon installation, any syscall not explicitly permitted triggers the kernel to terminate the process, thus preventing arbitrary or malicious kernel exploitation beyond the sanctioned operations.

Linux Namespaces: Controlling Process Visibility

and Capabilities

Linux namespaces provide isolation of kernel resources, offering processes distinct views and control spaces. Namespaces relevant to sandboxing include:

- **PID namespace**: Isolates process ID number space, preventing sandboxed processes from seeing or affecting processes outside the namespace.

- **Mount namespace**: Provides each sandboxed environment its own filesystem hierarchy, enabling containment of filesystem views.

- **Network namespace**: Creates separate networking stacks, interfaces, routing tables, and firewall rules.

- **User namespace**: Maps user and group IDs such that processes can run as root inside the namespace without real root privileges outside.

- **IPC and UTS namespaces**: Isolate interprocess communication and system identifiers (hostname, domainname).

Establishing these namespaces creates a confined context in which the process operates, providing strong protection from interactions with the host or other system processes. For example, to create a new mount and PID namespace combined with user namespace mapping a non-root host user to root inside the sandbox, one might use the `clone()` system call with appropriate flags:

```
#define STACK_SIZE (1024 * 1024)
char child_stack[STACK_SIZE];

int child_func(void *arg) {
    // Mount and PID namespace isolated code path
```

```
    // Setup root filesystem, drop privileges or remap
    UID
    // Run sandboxed workload
    return 0;
}

int main() {
    int flags = CLONE_NEWUSER | CLONE_NEWPID |
    CLONE_NEWNS | SIGCHLD;
    pid_t pid = clone(child_func, child_stack +
    STACK_SIZE, flags, NULL);
    if (pid == -1) {
        perror("clone");
        return 1;
    }
    waitpid(pid, NULL, 0);
    return 0;
}
```

Proper setup of user namespaces requires writing to /proc/[pid]/uid_map and /proc/[pid]/gid_map to map IDs post-fork. Mount namespaces often involve a pivot_root or chroot to a dedicated filesystem subtree containing only allowed binaries and resources.

Control Groups (cgroups): Enforcing Resource Limits

While namespaces isolate and confine a process's view, control groups (cgroups) manage and enforce resource usage limits, crucial for mitigating denial-of-service vectors from resource exhaustion or runaway processes.

Cgroups version 2 (cgroups v2) unified resource controllers, enabling fine-grained control over CPU, memory, I/O, and more. Relevant controllers for sandboxing include:

- cpu: Limits CPU time allocation.

- memory: Caps memory usage and can configure OOM behavior.

213

- `io`: Restricts block device I/O bandwidth.

- `pids`: Limits the maximum number of processes/-forks.

Typically, the sandbox manager creates a new cgroup under the unified hierarchy, moves the sandboxed process into it, then applies settings via the cgroup filesystem interface. For example, to limit memory to 256 MB and limit processes to 10:

```
mkdir /sys/fs/cgroup/sandbox
echo $$ > /sys/fs/cgroup/sandbox/cgroup.procs
echo 268435456 > /sys/fs/cgroup/sandbox/memory.max
echo 10 > /sys/fs/cgroup/sandbox/pids.max
```

Manipulation of cgroups can be performed programmatically by writing to these interface files or by using APIs like `libcgroup` or `systemd-run` for higher-level abstraction.

Integration: Constructing a Robust Sandboxed Environment

The power of resource sandboxing emerges from the integration of seccomp, namespaces, and cgroups, which together enforce:

- **Capability restriction**: Seccomp limits syscalls to prevent unsafe kernel interfaces.

- **Resource isolation**: Namespaces restrict process visibility and resource access.

- **Resource allocation**: Cgroups enforce quotas and fairness on resource usage.

Consider the use case of sandboxing an untrusted computation module. The host launches a new process with cloned namespaces, mounts a read-only root filesystem with only essential binaries, applies user namespace to permit unprivileged root inside the container, installs a seccomp filter that allows only expected system calls, and places the process in cgroups limiting memory, CPU, and process count. This approach prevents the sandboxed process from:

- Escalating privileges on the host.

- Accessing arbitrarily mounted filesystems or network interfaces.

- Escalating resource consumption that destabilizes the host.

- Executing kernel system calls that could compromise the host kernel.

Challenges and Best Practices

While effective, resource sandboxing demands careful configuration and monitoring:

- **Seccomp filter correctness**: Overly permissive filters weaken security, while overly restrictive rules can break functionality. Testing with comprehensive syscall tracing is advisable.

- **Namespace lifecycle management**: User namespace mapping requires appropriate privilege handling, and mount namespaces need proper setup of the root filesystem to avoid escaping attacks.

- **Cgroup resource calibration**: Limits must balance between security and performance to avoid unnecessary denials of service to legitimate workloads.

- **Combining with other security modules**: Sandboxing works best when complemented with Linux Security Modules (LSMs) such as SELinux or AppArmor, adding mandatory access controls.

Example: Minimal Sandbox Setup Script

Below is a conceptual shell script snippet illustrating the creation of a sandbox environment combining these elements:

```bash
#!/bin/bash

SANDBOX_ROOT="/sandbox/rootfs"
CGROUP_PATH="/sys/fs/cgroup/sandbox"

# Create cgroup and set resource limits
mkdir -p $CGROUP_PATH
echo $$ > $CGROUP_PATH/cgroup.procs
echo 500000000 > $CGROUP_PATH/memory.max     # 500MB
echo 50 > $CGROUP_PATH/pids.max              # max 50
    processes
echo 100000 > $CGROUP_PATH/cpu.max           # 10% of
    a CPU

# Unshare namespaces: user, pid, mount
unshare --fork --pid --mount --user --map-root-user \
    chroot $SANDBOX_ROOT /bin/bash

# Inside chroot:
# 1. Install seccomp filter programmatically or via
    wrapper
# 2. Run untrusted code
```

This script sets resource limits, uses unshare to isolate and map root user inside user namespace, and executes code in a restricted filesystem hierarchy. It provides a robust baseline for safe execution with resource constraints.

System resource sandboxing using seccomp, Linux namespaces, and cgroups provides a layered security posture essential for modern container runtimes, secure workload execution, and attack surface minimization within Linux systems. Mastery of these tools enables containment of untrusted code with fine-grained control over behavior and resource consumption, critical in multi-tenant and security-sensitive environments.

8.5. Automated Vulnerability and Compliance Scanning

Automated vulnerability and compliance scanning are integral components of modern cybersecurity operations, serving to detect weaknesses and ensure adherence to security policies across diverse IT environments. Integration of these scanning tools into operational workflows enables continuous visibility into security posture, timely remediation, and enforcement of organizational compliance standards. This section delineates the foundational practices and key considerations for embedding vulnerability scanners and compliance platforms within automated processes, emphasizing continuous auditing, real-time tracking of Common Vulnerabilities and Exposures (CVEs), and enforcement of security baselines across heterogeneous infrastructure fleets.

Integrating Vulnerability Scanners into DevOps and Security Workflows

The automation of vulnerability scanning requires a seamless interface between scanning tools and existing workflows, including continuous integration/continuous deployment (CI/CD) pipelines, configuration management, and security information and event management (SIEM) systems. Leveraging APIs provided by leading vulnerability scanners permits programmatic execution, retrieval of scan results, and initiation of follow-up actions such as alerting or ticket creation.

A common integration involves embedding static and dynamic application security testing (SAST and DAST) scanners into CI/CD pipelines to inspect code and deployed applications automatically. For infrastructure, agent-based or agentless scanners can be scheduled to run prior to deployment or periodically during runtime, delivering reports that can be parsed and correlated with existing asset inventories.

The following example demonstrates automated execution of an open-source vulnerability scanner, such as OpenVAS, via its command-line interface within a scripted workflow:

```bash
#!/bin/bash
# Trigger OpenVAS full network scan
openvas-cli --start-scan --target 192.168.1.0/24 --
    profile Full-and-Fast --output scan_results.xml

# Parse and alert based on severity
high_vulns=$(grep -c "<severity>High</severity>"
    scan_results.xml)
if [[ $high_vulns -gt 0 ]]; then
  echo "High severity vulnerabilities detected:
    $high_vulns"
  # Integration point for alerting or creating incident
    tickets
fi
```

Such automation enables vulnerability detection to occur early and often, facilitating rapid feedback loops to developers and system administrators.

Continuous Auditing and Compliance Enforcement

Continuous auditing extends beyond periodic scans to incorporate real-time or near-real-time monitoring of compliance status. This is achieved by systematically collecting configuration data, security logs, and vulnerability findings, then applying predefined compliance rules to detect deviations from mandated baselines.

Compliance frameworks such as CIS Benchmarks, NIST standards, and industry-specific regulations define security baselines that can be codified within audit tools like OpenSCAP, Chef InSpec, or commercial platforms. These tools often provide declarative profiles that describe required system states, and their integration into orchestrated workflows enables automated remediation or blocking of non-compliant configurations.

Automated compliance enforcement relies on tight feedback loops among scanning tools, configuration management systems, and workload orchestration layers. For example, when an audit tool detects a deviation from the established baseline on a cloud instance, an automation engine can trigger a remediation playbook to correct the setting or quarantine the resource until compliance is restored.

An abstracted flow of continuous auditing and enforcement can be captured as:

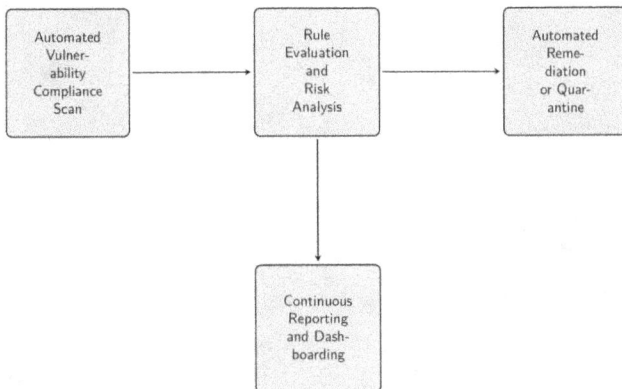

Tracking and Managing CVEs Across Infrastructure Fleets

The dynamic nature of IT ecosystems necessitates robust mechanisms for tracking and managing CVEs as new vulnerabilities are disclosed. Given that CVE databases are updated rapidly and often, automated ingestion pipelines for these feeds such as the National Vulnerability Database (NVD), vendor advisories, or commercial threat intelligence services are essential.

Correlating CVEs with asset inventories and scan results enables prioritization of remediation efforts based on exploitability, asset criticality, and operational context. This correlation may be performed by vulnerability management platforms, which maintain mappings between package versions, installed software, and known CVEs.

A practical approach to continuous CVE tracking involves scheduling periodic vulnerability data updates, reconciling these with scan outputs, and triggering automated patch management or risk acceptance workflows. The process can be represented algorithmically as follows:

Algorithm 1 CVE Tracking and Remediation Prioritization

1: **Input:** AssetInventory, LatestCVEs, ScanFindings
2: **Output:** PrioritizedRemediationList
3:
4: **function** UpdateVulnerabilityDatabase(LatestCVEs)
5:     Fetch and parse new CVE data
6:     Update local vulnerability repository
7: **end function**
8:
9: **function** MatchScanFindings(ScanFindings, Asset-Inventory)
10:     Map vulnerabilities to specific assets and installed software versions
11: **end function**
12:
13: **function** PrioritizeRemediations(MatchedFindings)
14:     Assign risk scores based on CVE severity, asset criticality, and exploit availability
15:     Sort vulnerabilities by descending risk
16:     **return** PrioritizedRemediationList
17: **end function**
18:
19: UpdateVulnerabilityDatabase(LatestCVEs)
20: MatchedFindings ← MatchScanFindings(ScanFindings, AssetInventory)
21: PrioritizedRemediationList ← PrioritizeRemediations(MatchedFindings)
22: **return** PrioritizedRemediationList

Integration with patch management and change control systems permits automated or semi-automated deployment of fixes, reducing dwell time and exposure. Additionally, dashboards and alerting mechanisms provide secu-

221

rity teams continuous situational awareness and reporting capabilities.

Enforcing Security Baselines at Scale

Enforcement of security baselines across extensive fleets requires consistent configuration management and policy adherence across heterogeneous operating systems and environments. Centralized management platforms facilitate this by applying uniform policies through configuration-as-code paradigms.

Configuration management tools such as Ansible, Puppet, or Chef are commonly paired with compliance scanning utilities to implement and verify required system states. For cloud-native environments, infrastructure-as-code tools like Terraform integrate with compliance scanners to validate desired state before resource provisioning.

Policies encoded as baseline profiles can express settings such as password complexity, network firewall rules, installed software versions, or auditing configurations. Continuous enforcement is achieved via scheduled scans combined with configuration drift detection and automated remediation.

For example, enforcing a CIS security benchmark on Linux servers may involve the following command sequence using OpenSCAP:

```
# Evaluate system against the CIS profile
oscap xccdf eval --profile cis --results report.xml /usr
    /share/xml/scap/ssg/content/ssg-centos7-ds.xml

# Generate human-readable report
oscap xccdf generate report report.xml -o
    compliance_report.html

# Apply remediation (if applicable)
oscap xccdf generate fix report.xml -o remediation.sh
bash remediation.sh
```

The ability to generate remediation scripts automatically accelerates corrective action while maintaining audit trails. Combining such tooling with orchestration frameworks enables scaling enforcement across thousands of endpoints with minimal manual intervention.

Challenges and Best Practices

Key challenges in automated vulnerability and compliance scanning include managing false positives, ensuring scan coverage, handling credential management securely, and aligning scan schedules to minimize operational disruption. Balancing thoroughness with efficiency necessitates tuning scanner configurations and selectively scanning critical assets more frequently.

Best practices encompass:

- Integrating scanning tools early in development pipelines to shift security left.

- Maintaining up-to-date vulnerability databases and compliance profiles.

- Correlating scan data with asset inventories for precise risk prioritization.

- Ensuring remediation workflows are clearly defined and automated where feasible.

- Leveraging role-based access controls to limit exposure of scanning credentials.

- Employing centralized reporting to unify visibility across tooling heterogeneity.

Through strategic automation, continuous auditing, and rigorous baseline enforcement, organizations can dramatically enhance their resilience against evolving threats

while meeting regulatory expectations and internal security mandates.

8.6. Incident Detection and Response

Effective incident detection and response within minimal
Alpine Linux environments demands strategies optimized
for constrained system resources and minimal service footprints. Alpine's lean design simplifies attack surfaces but
necessitates precise tooling and methodology to promptly
identify, contain, and remediate threats without reliance
on heavyweight security frameworks. This section elucidates actionable approaches employing Alpine-native utilities to build resilient real-time detection, rapid lockdown,
forensic analysis, and recovery workflows.

Real-Time Threat Detection Strategies

Alpine's foundation on BusyBox and musl libc allows integration of lightweight monitoring tools that leverage
kernel-level event notifications and simple log correlation.
The primary objective is to acquire timely indicators of
compromise while minimizing performance overhead.

The auditd framework, configurable through
/etc/audit/audit.rules, provides kernel auditing
capabilities enabling monitoring of system calls and file
accesses critical for detecting unauthorized actions. A
minimalist rule set might include watches on sensitive
paths such as:

```
-w /etc/shadow -p wa -k shadow-modification
-w /var/log/auth.log -p wa -k auth-log
-w /usr/bin -p x -k exec-watch
```

These directives log write and attribute changes to
/etc/shadow, authentication event logs, and execution of

binaries respectively. Events surface anomalies such as privilege escalation attempts or log tampering.

Alpine's default syslog daemon, busybox syslogd, can be configured to relay selective logs to a dedicated monitoring host using tcp or udp transport. This isolation supports real-time aggregation with correlation engines external to the target system, enhancing detection fidelity without burdening the local machine.

Complementing auditd, periodic invocation of cryptographic integrity checks is crucial. Alpine's minimal package manager apk includes capabilities to verify installed file hashes, usable to signal unauthorized modifications by comparing baseline manifests created after system hardening. For example:

```
apk verify | grep -v 'OK'
```

This command outputs any file diverging from its authenticated package checksum, promptly alerting administrators of potential compromise.

Rapid Lockdown Techniques

Upon detection of suspicious activity, swift containment limits attacker mobility and preserves volatile evidence. Alpine's small footprint restricts elaborate containment workflows; instead, immediate measures focus on network isolation, process suspension, and selective access control.

First, network lockdown is achieved by dynamically enforcing firewall policies using iptables, which is natively available:

```
iptables -P INPUT DROP
iptables -P FORWARD DROP
iptables -P OUTPUT DROP
iptables -A INPUT -i lo -j ACCEPT
iptables -A OUTPUT -o lo -j ACCEPT
```

This sequence blocks all external connectivity except the loopback interface, isolating the system from lateral threats. Administrators may selectively open minimal ports to maintain essential communication.

Second, suspicious or unknown processes can be swiftly paused or terminated by leveraging `pkill` and `kill` commands filtered by user, name, or behavior:

```
pkill -STOP -u attacker_user
```

Suspending processes rather than immediate termination preserves runtime state for subsequent forensic analysis.

Third, file system restrictions utilize `chattr` and `mount` options to prevent further tampering. Mounting key directories as read-only can be performed via:

```
mount -o remount,ro /etc
```

This reduces further modification risk, containing the spread of malware artifacts.

Playbook-Driven Incident Response

Given Alpine's streamlined environment, incident response benefits from standardized playbooks encoded as shell scripts, orchestrating detection, lockdown, and logging procedures. A modular playbook ensures rapid repeatability and consistent response across deployments.

An example playbook segment for detection is:

```
#!/bin/sh
auditctl -D
auditctl -w /etc/shadow -p wa -k shadow-watch
auditctl -w /var/log/auth.log -p wa -k auth-watch
syslogd -r 514 &
```

Further contain and analyze functionalities can be appended as the incident escalates, including network lockdown and cryptographic hash comparisons.

Embedding detailed documentation within scripts ensures maintainability, while advocating automating evidence collection steps-copying audit logs, exporting process snapshots (via `ps aux`), and capturing network states (`iptables-save`)-for prompt forensic evaluation.

Forensic Analysis in Minimal Systems

Post-incident forensics emphasize evidence preservation and detailed insight into attack vectors within resource-limited Alpine hosts. Essential artifacts for examination include audit logs, system logs, process trees, loaded kernel modules, and file integrity manifests.

Utilizing `ausearch` to parse audit logs enables pinpointing suspicious events:

```
ausearch -k shadow-watch -ts recent
```

This extracts recent modifications corresponding to critical files. Supplementary analysis employs `strace` or `lsof` on paused processes to understand attacker operations when live response is possible.

Core dumps and memory snapshots are challenging on minimal systems; however, saving `/proc` entries provides incomplete but valuable runtime metadata:

```
cp -r /proc/<pid> /var/forensics/
```

Immutable storage of collected evidence on external media ensures data integrity for offline examination.

Recovery and Remediation Processes

Alpine's package-oriented architecture simplifies system recovery by restoring verified binaries and configurations using apk. Full reinstallation of compromised packages ensures removal of malicious binaries:

```
apk fix --force
```

Alternatively, rebuilding the system from a known-good snapshot or container image is often expedient.

Recovery procedures must include resetting credentials and key material compromised during the incident. Regeneration of SSH keys and password updates should be scripted and automated as part of the remediation phase.

Finally, hardening the system against future incidents utilizes kernel-level security modules such as `grsecurity` patches or AppArmor, where applicable, alongside tightened audit rules and proactive log monitoring.

The iterative practice of refining detection rules, updating playbooks based on attack intelligence, and conducting drills ensures Alpine deployments achieve robust incident readiness despite their inherent minimalism.

Chapter 9

System Diagnostics, Troubleshooting, and Recovery

The health and reliability of an Alpine Linux system depend not only on how it's built—but on your ability to swiftly diagnose and solve problems when things go awry. This chapter is a toolkit for the vigilant operator: empowering you to dig deep, trace elusive faults, optimize performance, and recover from disasters with clarity and confidence. Through step-by-step approaches and real-world scenarios, learn how to turn setbacks into opportunities for resilience and mastery over even the most challenging failures.

9.1. Boot Process Debugging

The Alpine Linux boot process begins with firmware execution, typically UEFI or BIOS, which initializes the platform to a known state and loads the bootloader, commonly `syslinux`, `grub`, or `extlinux` depending on the system configuration. This stage is responsible for launching the Linux kernel and its initial RAM filesystem (initramfs). Understanding the interaction among these components is critical for effective debugging of boot failures.

The firmware primarily initializes hardware and prepares the system to load the bootloader from a predefined storage device. Failures here often prevent even the first bootloader prompt from appearing. Diagnosis includes examining firmware settings, verifying boot device order, and using vendor diagnostic utilities. Debugging early failures may also require connecting to a serial console if available, capturing early firmware messages, or employing firmware recovery mechanisms.

Once the bootloader gains control, it loads the kernel and initramfs image(s) into memory. The bootloader configuration-usually found at `/boot/grub/grub.cfg` or `/boot/syslinux/syslinux.cfg`-defines kernel parameters, such as the `root` device and options like `quiet` or `console`. Misconfigured kernel command lines are a frequent cause of boot problems. It is recommended to remove or reduce verbosity-controlling options and add `loglevel=7` for maximum kernel message output during troubleshooting. Additionally, specifying `console=ttyS0,115200` (adjusted to the system's serial port) directs kernel messages to the serial console, enabling remote capture of early issues.

The Linux kernel is then decompressed and initialized.

Key steps include hardware detection, device driver loading, and mounting the root filesystem, usually passed from the initramfs environment. Kernel panics represent critical errors detected by the kernel that halt system initialization. Common causes include incompatible kernel modules, misconfigured hardware parameters, missing root filesystems, or corrupted kernel images. Parsing kernel panic messages is essential; they often contain indicator strings such as `Kernel panic - not syncing:` followed by the specific fault. Using a serial console or netconsole is invaluable for capturing kernel output that otherwise disappears after system halt.

The initramfs, a temporary root filesystem loaded into memory, plays a pivotal role by providing the necessary executables and scripts to mount the actual root filesystem. Alpine's initramfs is typically generated via `mkinitfs` and includes scripts in `/etc/init.d/` or `/etc/conf.d/` that configure storage, load kernel modules, check filesystems, and handle encryption or logical volume management setups. A corrupted or incorrectly built initramfs results in early userspace failures and may cause the kernel to drop into the initramfs shell if configured. Common troubleshooting steps include regenerating the initramfs image, verifying the `init` script's executability and syntax, and ensuring the root device is correctly referenced.

For diagnostic access during boot failures related to initramfs or kernel parameters, Alpine supports recovery modes and emergency shells. Passing the `break` parameter on the kernel command line instructs the initramfs scripts to pause, presenting an interactive shell before mounting the root filesystem. This environment allows manual inspection of device nodes, kernel modules, logs (e.g., `/proc/kmsg`), and filesystem check commands such as `fsck`. Recovery shells may also be accessed by pressing keys during bootloader time, depending on configuration, or by booting from a live Alpine ISO image.

Troubleshooting boot failures commonly follows a systematic approach:

1. **Capture Early Boot Logs:** Redirect console output to serial or VGA to observe kernel messages, firmware handshakes, and bootloader activity.

2. **Check Bootloader Configuration:** Confirm kernel and initramfs paths, root filesystem parameters, and appropriateness of kernel command line flags.

3. **Isolate Kernel Issues:** Boot with a known good kernel version, disable extraneous modules, and increase log verbosity.

4. **Verify Initramfs Integrity:** Regenerate initramfs, confirm scripts within are executable and error-free, and ensure dependencies (e.g., device drivers, cryptsetup) match the hardware.

5. **Utilize Recovery Shells:** Use break or emergency boot options to inspect mounted devices and locate failed mounts or filesystem corruption.

6. **Analyze Kernel Panics:** Study kernel panic stacks and oops messages, searching for common patterns such as missing modules, bad memory addresses, or hardware incompatibilities.

7. **Leverage External Tools:** Use serial consoles, USB-to-serial adapters, JTAG debuggers, and netboot environments to gain in-depth access when local outputs are insufficient.

When persistent boot failures occur, a useful method is to live boot the Alpine installation media and chroot into the installed system. This facilitates repair of critical files such as /etc/fstab, kernel parameters, or the initramfs config-uration. Additionally, rebuilding the kernel or reinstalling the bootloader can resolve corruption-related failures.

Debugging the Alpine Linux boot process requires compre-hensive understanding of each stage-from firmware inter-actions through kernel loading to early userspace initial-ization. Systematic isolation of failure points, thorough analysis of verbose boot messages, and mastery of recov-ery utilities enable administrators to restore systems ef-ficiently. Access to recovery shells early in the boot se-quence is an essential tool, allowing hands-on diagnosis of hardware, kernel, and filesystem issues that underlie most boot-time failures.

9.2. Performance Monitoring and Pro-filing

Low-level performance monitoring constitutes a founda-tional practice for identifying and resolving system ineffi-ciencies at the hardware and operating system levels. Pre-cise bottleneck detection in CPU, memory, disk, and net-work subsystems is essential for optimizing workload ex-ecution, improving throughput, and minimizing latency. This section explicates the application of key tools—top, htop, nmon, and eBPF (extended Berkeley Packet Filter)—to systematically measure resource utilization and profile system behavior. Emphasis is placed on leveraging col-lected metrics for data-driven performance tuning.

top is a widely available command-line utility providing a real-time, dynamic view of running processes, along with CPU and memory usage. Its default display ranks pro-cesses by CPU consumption, revealing hot spots in CPU utilization. The persistent updating mode, coupled with information on load averages and CPU wait times, makes top a useful first step for detecting CPU saturation or runaway processes. However, top lacks advanced interactivity and detailed subsystem metrics.

Enhancing top's capabilities, htop offers a more user-friendly, ncurses-based interface with color coding and intuitive keyboard navigation. It visualizes CPU core load distributions individually, exposing imbalances or core contention not evident in top. The integrated meters for memory, swap, and I/O rates provide a consolidated overview of system health. Filters and tree views allow exploration of process hierarchies, enabling correlation of resource spikes with specific workloads.

The nmon (network, memory, and CPU monitor) tool extends monitoring breadth, offering a comprehensive real-time dashboard that captures CPU, memory, disk I/O, network traffic, and filesystem utilization. Unlike top and htop, nmon aggregates long-term performance data in downloadable files, facilitating post-mortem analysis and trend identification. Metrics such as disk queue length and CPU run queue length pinpoint hardware-level bottlenecks. Network module statistics, including interface errors and packet rates, assist in isolating communication bottlenecks.

While these traditional monitoring utilities provide valuable snapshots and trend data, modern complex workloads require fine-grained, event-driven profiling. The extended Berkeley Packet Filter (eBPF) framework enables custom instrumentation within the Linux kernel without recompilation or downtime. eBPF facilitates dynamic tracing of events, system calls, and kernel functions, with minimal overhead. Tools built on eBPF, such as bcc and

bpftrace, allow targeted analysis of CPU scheduling delays, cache misses, system call latencies, and network
packet flow at an unparalleled resolution.

For example, the following bpftrace script traces CPU off-
CPU time—a key indicator of scheduling contention:

```
tracepoint:sched:sched_switch
{
    @offcpu[comm] = hist(nsecs / 1000000);
}
```

The resulting histogram quantifies per-process delays
while waiting for CPU resumption, guiding identification
of processes experiencing starvation or causing
contention.

Effective profiling begins with establishing baseline performance metrics under typical load conditions. Utilizing htop or nmon, analysts can observe overall system resource usage and detect anomalies in CPU load distribution, memory pressure, or I/O bottlenecks. If CPU saturation is observed, the next step is to determine whether it
results from user-space compute, kernel-space overhead,
or specific system calls. Employing eBPF-based tools enables this fine-grained inspection, tracing processor cycles
spent in various execution contexts.

Memory bottlenecks typically manifest as excessive swap
activity or page faults. Monitoring virtual memory statistics via vmstat in conjunction with nmon disk and memory modules can corroborate memory exhaustion hypothe-
ses. eBPF probes targeting page fault handlers reveal exact faulting processes and access patterns—crucial for optimizing memory allocations or adjusting working set sizes.

Disk I/O contention is surfaced by increased queue
lengths and wait times observable through nmon's storage
metrics or iostat. High disk latency may necessitate

235

cataloging command latencies and identifying process-level I/O hotspots. eBPF tools instrumenting block-layer queues provide these insights without imposing kernel reloads.

Network performance degradation often correlates with interface errors, dropped packets, or saturated transmit queues. nmon network metrics highlight interface health, while eBPF network tracers correlate packet flows with process identities and protocol-level events. Such information is pivotal when troubleshooting microservice communication delays or abnormal retransmissions.

Data collected through these layered monitoring techniques supports quantitative, hypothesis-driven performance improvements. For instance, if profiling reveals CPU bottlenecks in kernel space due to frequent context switches, tuning scheduler parameters or reducing interrupt frequency may be warranted. Excessive memory swapping suggests reallocation of application memory limits or physical memory expansion. Disk I/O saturation could be alleviated by load balancing across storage devices or employing caching mechanisms. Network packet loss or latency call for examining interface configurations, driver updates, or quality of service (QoS) policies.

The iterative workflow of monitoring, profiling, analyzing, and tuning benefits from automation via scripts and dashboards, enabling continuous performance assessment and immediate alerting on regressions. Combining real-time utilities (htop, nmon) for ongoing observation with event-driven tracing (eBPF) for root-cause analysis achieves a holistic understanding of system behavior.

Mastering these performance monitoring tools and profiling methodologies equips practitioners to accurately pinpoint subsystem bottlenecks and to implement targeted, data-backed optimizations. This foundation is indispensable for maintaining robust, efficient computing environments amid increasingly complex workload demands.

9.3. Detecting and Resolving Package and Dependency Failures

Package management systems are critical in maintaining software consistency, yet they often face challenges such as conflicts, broken dependencies, and integration issues that may disrupt system stability. In the context of apk, the Alpine Linux package manager, effective strategies for detecting and resolving these failures are essential for maintaining reliable system environments.

Package conflicts typically arise when two or more packages attempt to install files at the same path or when incompatible versions of packages are required simultaneously by different dependencies. Broken dependencies occur when a package requires other packages or versions that are not installed, have been removed, or have been upgraded to incompatible versions. Integration issues often manifest as runtime errors or malfunctioning services following package upgrades, pointing to subtle incompatibilities.

Detecting Package Conflicts and Broken Dependencies

The initial step in diagnosing package-related failures is thorough log analysis. The apk tool generates logs during package installation, upgrade, and removal operations, accessible through the system's journaling facilities or specific package logs. These logs often contain error messages such as missing dependencies (unsatisfied dependencies), file collisions, or version mismatches.

For example, the command

```
apk add --update mypackage
```

may yield errors such as:

```
ERROR: unsatisfiable constraints:
  dependency1 (missing):
    required by: mypackage-1.0.0-r0
    conflict: file collision: /usr/bin/tool1 exists in file system
```

This clearly indicates a missing dependency and a file collision, providing a basis for remediation.

The apk info command assists in examining installed packages and their files, enabling identification of overlapping files between packages:

```
apk info -L conflictingpackage
```

This lists files managed by conflictingpackage, aiding in pinpointing the source of file collisions.

The apk fix command attempts to repair packages with broken dependencies or partial installations, downloading required packages or correcting incomplete states. However, apk fix requires a correctly configured repository environment and network connectivity.

Resolving Package Conflicts

When file collisions occur, practical strategies depend on the context of the conflict. If two packages unintentionally share files, one approach is to evaluate which package is essential for the target application. Removing or replacing the conflicting package with an appropriately versioned or patched alternative can reduce collisions.

In cases where files legitimately overlap, such as common

utilities included by multiple packages, merging packages into a meta-package or modifying package scripts to avoid duplicate files may be necessary.

Alternatively, apk supports the --force-overwrite option to forcibly replace conflicting files during installation. This method should be applied cautiously:

```
apk add --force-overwrite conflictingpackage
```

While this may resolve the immediate conflict, it risks overwriting critical files and introducing system instability.

Handling Dependency Failures

Broken dependencies necessitate verifying the current state of repositories and package databases. Synchronizing the local package index with remote repositories via

```
apk update
```

is fundamental to ensure up-to-date dependency resolution.

In cases where dependency versions have shifted or packages have been removed from repositories, pinning specific package versions in the apk configuration can maintain compatibility. This is achieved by specifying package versions explicitly:

```
apk add package=1.2.3-r0
```

Alternatively, if local sources or custom repositories are maintained, verifying their consistency and integrity is vital.

For corrupted or partially installed packages, removing problematic packages using

```
apk del problematicpackage
```

followed by a clean installation often restores a consistent state.

Integration Issue Diagnostics

Integration failures may not always manifest as direct package manager errors but can impact services or applications. System logs, accessible via dmesg, journalctl, or application-specific log files, must be analyzed for segmentation faults, missing shared libraries, or startup failures.

Dynamic linking issues often stem from incompatible library versions or missing runtime dependencies. Verifying installed shared libraries and their versions with

```
ldd /path/to/executable
```

and correlating with apk info can identify discrepancies.

Rebuilding packages from source with consistent build flags or updating packages to versions compatible with the current system environment is a systematic resolution approach.

Rollback and Safe State Restoration

Proactive management of package states is essential to limit downtime. apk does not natively support full transaction rollbacks; however, layering strategies and metadata snapshots can serve this purpose.

Creating snapshots of installed package states can be accomplished by exporting the list of currently installed packages:

```
apk info -vv | awk '{print $1}' > installed_packages.
    list
```

Subsequent restoration after a failed upgrade or installation is performed by reinstalling the recorded packages:

```
apk del --purge $(apk info -vv | awk '{print $1}')
```

```
apk add $(cat installed_packages.list)
```

For more comprehensive rollback, employing system-level snapshot tools such as btrfs or LVM snapshots complements apk's capabilities by capturing full system states.

Logging detailed information during package operations enables targeted rollbacks by identifying exact package versions and modification timestamps.

Best Practices for Prevention

To minimize package and dependency conflicts, enforcing strict version control and repository curation is critical. Maintaining custom or vetted repositories ensures compatibility and reduces unexpected removals or upgrades.

Automated continuous integration pipelines that validate package installation, upgrade, and removal sequences help detect inconsistencies before deployment. Incorporating integration tests that mimic production environments allows early identification of latent conflicts.

Documenting package dependencies and configuration changes supports efficient troubleshooting and rollback procedures.

Combining systematic logging, careful dependency management, controlled package installations, and leveraging system snapshots forms a robust framework for detecting and resolving package and dependency failures in apk-managed systems.

9.4. Network Diagnostics and Packet Tracing

Effective network diagnostics and packet tracing are indispensable in modern network management, enabling detailed inspection, real-time analysis, and resolution of complex connectivity issues. This section explores advanced methodologies for employing tcpdump, Wireshark, netcat, and nmap-four pivotal tools for network professionals.

tcpdump operates at the packet-capture level, providing command-line access to raw network traffic. Its filtering syntax, based on Berkeley Packet Filter (BPF) expressions, allows precise isolation of protocol types, IP addresses, ports, and packet flags. For example, to capture only TCP SYN packets directed to a web server for SSH troubleshooting, one can invoke:

```
tcpdump -i eth0 'tcp[tcpflags] & tcp-syn != 0 and dst
    port 22'
```

This command filters the TCP header flags to identify SYN packets, isolating connection initiation attempts. Employing verbose output flags -v, -vv, or -vvv enriches packet detail, aiding in identifying retransmissions, sequence anomalies, or unexpected flag combinations.

Wireshark extends functionality into a graphical domain, offering sophisticated dissection capabilities. It supports multi-layer inspection, decoding application-layer protocols such as HTTP/2, TLS, and DNS, with color-coded packet categorization. Captured packets are indexed and time-stamped, facilitating temporal analysis of interactions and round-trip times (RTT). Applying display filters, for example:

```
http.request.method == "POST" && ip.addr ==
```

242

```
192.168.1.100
```

pinpoints HTTP POST requests from a specified host. The protocol hierarchy statistics further assist in overviewing traffic distribution, highlighting potential bottlenecks or unauthorized protocol usage.

On troubleshooting connectivity, a typical workflow integrates tcpdump and Wireshark. Begin by capturing traffic at the suspected network interface during issue replication with tcpdump, ensuring minimal performance impact and file size control through options such as -c (capture count) and -w (write to file). The resulting capture file is subsequently loaded into Wireshark for detailed analysis. Leveraging Wireshark's follow-stream functionality can reconstruct entire TCP sessions, revealing packet losses, resets, or malformed segments.

netcat (often abbreviated nc) complements packet analysis by providing network connectivity testing and data transfer capabilities. Acting as both a client and a server, netcat can probe services and validate firewall rules or port listening states. For instance, to test a TCP port, the command

```
nc -vz example.com 80
```

performs a TCP connect scan, printing the status of the connection attempt. The -z flag ensures no data is sent, focusing solely on port availability. For interactive diagnostics, netcat can be used to send arbitrary data or scripts over TCP or UDP, assisting in service behavior validation or basic throughput measurement.

In complex scenarios involving host discovery and security auditing, nmap exhibits unparalleled flexibility. Its wide repertoire of scanning techniques-SYN scan (-sS), TCP connect scan (-sT), UDP scan (-sU)-supports stealth and comprehensive reconnaissance. For example, a SYN scan with version detection and OS fingerprinting is executed by:

```
nmap -sS -sV -O 192.168.1.0/24
```

This scans an entire subnet, identifying open ports, service versions, and probable operating systems, enabling targeted troubleshooting or vulnerability assessment. Integrating timing options (-T4, -T5) adjusts scan speed, balancing thoroughness against network load and stealth.

Real-world troubleshooting often requires orchestrating these tools in a coordinated flow. Consider a scenario where a web application intermittently fails to connect to its backend database. Initial steps include:

- Executing an nmap scan on the database server's IP to verify open ports and services:

```
nmap -p 5432 -sV db-server.example.com
```

- Using netcat from the application server to test TCP connectivity to port 5432:

```
nc -vz db-server.example.com 5432
```

- Capturing network packets on both the application and database servers during failure occurrences with tcpdump:

```
tcpdump -i eth0 host db-server.example.com and
        port 5432 -w capture.pcap
```

- Analyzing the tcpdump capture in Wireshark to detect TCP retransmissions, resets, or anomalies in handshake processes.

Such a structured approach elucidates whether connectivity issues stem from firewall blocks, service downtime, packet loss, or misconfigured network policies.

Packet-level inspection frequently reveals subtle issues invisible to higher-level diagnostics. For example, inspecting TCP sequence numbers and acknowledgments can expose packet reordering or duplication, manifestations of network congestion or faulty hardware. Additionally, examination of TLS handshakes in Wireshark may uncover certificate mismatches or protocol downgrading attempts, critical in securing enterprise environments.

Advanced filtering techniques in tcpdump employ compound expressions with logical operators, enabling fine-grained capture rules. For example:

```
tcpdump '((src net 10.0.0.0/24 and dst port 443) or (dst
    net 10.0.1.0/24 and src port 80))'
```

captures HTTPS traffic initiated from one subnet and HTTP responses from another, useful in multi-segment troubleshooting.

Understanding the temporal relationship of packets, including inter-packet delays, is facilitated by Wireshark's time delta columns, essential for diagnosing latency issues or microbursts. Moreover, Wireshark supports Lua scripting for custom dissections and automated alerts, enabling scalability in complex network environments.

Proficiency in leveraging tcpdump, Wireshark, netcat, and nmap transforms network diagnostics from reactive measures into proactive incident analysis frameworks. Mastery of these tools' advanced capabilities and their methodical application is fundamental to achieving rapid fault isolation and effective remediation in increasingly heterogeneous and high-performance network infrastructures.

9.5. Filesystem Consistency and Recovery

Filesystems are foundational to data integrity, providing structured storage and retrieval mechanisms. However, unpredictable events such as unexpected shutdowns, hardware faults, or software bugs can lead to filesystem corruption. Ensuring filesystem consistency requires both proactive integrity verification and reactive recovery techniques. This section examines established methods for maintaining filesystem health, focusing on usage and implementation of `fsck` utilities across common formats including ext4, f2fs, btrfs, and overlayfs, followed by practical approaches to data recovery and preventive strategies against future faults.

Filesystem Health Verification Using `fsck`

The `fsck` (file system consistency check) utility is the primary tool for detecting and repairing inconsistencies in Unix-like filesystems. It operates by validating metadata structures such as inodes, directory entries, and allocation bitmaps against the expected properties defined by the filesystem's format.

For **ext4**, `fsck.ext4` examines the superblock, group descriptors, inode tables, and block bitmaps. Typical corruption markers include invalid inode link counts, orphaned inodes, and inconsistent block allocations. The command

```
sudo fsck.ext4 -v /dev/sdXN
```

invokes a verbose check that guides through repair prompts or, optionally, repairs automatically with the -y flag. The ext4 journaling mechanism mitigates many inconsistencies by replaying journals on mount, but `fsck.ext4` becomes necessary when journal recovery is insufficient.

The **flash-friendly filesystem (f2fs)** employs a log-structured design optimized for NAND flash storage. fsck.f2fs verifies segment summaries, node and checkpoint areas, and validity of allocation tables:

```
sudo fsck.f2fs /dev/sdXN
```

Its ability to repair corrupted checkpoint packs is critical to restoring consistency. Due to f2fs's append-only nature, inconsistencies mainly arise from sudden power loss before checkpoint commits.

Btrfs integrates advanced features such as checksumming, copy-on-write, and multi-device support, complicating traditional repair paradigms. The btrfs check utility provides a read-only or repair mode:

```
sudo btrfs check --repair /dev/sdXN
```

However, the repair flag should be used cautiously, as aggressive modifications can exacerbate damage. Btrfs's checksums allow detection of silent data corruptions, enabling partial recovery from bit-rot by substituting intact copies from replicas or RAID arrays when available.

OverlayFS is a stackable filesystem primarily used for container environments. It combines a read-only lower filesystem with a writable upper filesystem. Conventional fsck tools are generally applied to the underlying filesystems, since OverlayFS itself does not maintain independent on-disk metadata that requires consistency checking. Care must be taken when using fsck on the lower or upper layers to ensure that no active mounts interfere with the operation.

Recovery Techniques for Lost or Corrupted Data

Recovering lost data depends on the nature and extent

of corruption. For ext4, `extundelete` and `debugfs` are prominent tools for inode-level recovery. `debugfs` provides interactive filesystem access to locate and salvage orphaned files:

```
sudo debugfs /dev/sdXN
```

Within `debugfs`, commands such as `lsdel` (list deleted inodes) and `dump` (copy file contents) facilitate targeted recovery.

In the case of f2fs, due to its log-structured design, recovery is inherently more challenging. However, `f2fs-tools` incorporates repair mechanisms to restore segment validity. Use of `f2fsck` with options to perform forensic recovery should be prioritized only after standard `fsck` approaches fail.

Btrfs's built-in snapshotting capabilities offer unparalleled opportunities for data restoration. Snapshots can be mounted read-only or cloned to revert to previous states. When metadata is corrupted, `btrfs restore` attempts to recover files from damaged filesystems by scanning for file contents directly from blocks:

```
sudo btrfs restore -v -t 500 /dev/sdXN /mnt/recovery/
```

The -t option limits the amount of data restored; this tunable parameter allows partial recovery even from severely impacted volumes.

In overlay or containerized environments using OverlayFS, recovery is more complex due to layered structures. Persistent storage of the upper layer and periodic snapshots of the lower layer mitigate risks. Leveraging container-specific backup solutions aligned with the overlay approach proves more effective than direct filesystem-level recovery.

Preventing Future Integrity Issues

Preventive measures are essential to maintaining filesystem consistency and improving resilience. Journaling and copy-on-write mechanisms, as implemented in ext4 and btrfs respectively, form the first line of defense. Tuning mount options such as data=journal for ext4 improves consistency guarantees at a performance cost.

Regularly scheduled filesystem scans using non-invasive fsck checks can detect latent corruption, avoiding catastrophic failures. Integration of SMART (Self-Monitoring, Analysis, and Reporting Technology) tools into system health monitoring anticipates hardware degradation that precipitates filesystem issues.

Prudent use of snapshots and incremental backups forms a redundancy layer. Btrfs snapshots facilitate real-time rollback options, while higher-level scripts can automate these operations, reducing manual intervention.

For flash-based media formatted with f2fs, ensuring stable power supply and leveraging kernel-level write barriers and checkpoint intervals reduce corruption probability. User-space utilities for preemptive scrubbing detect and correct inconsistencies before manifest corruption.

Additionally, avoiding unclean shutdowns through UPS (Uninterruptible Power Supplies) and disabling forced reboots improves the reliability of all filesystem types. Equally important is the avoidance of forced fsck bypass during boot sequences, except in recovery scenarios, to safeguard consistent states.

Summary of Best Practices

- Invoke fsck regularly, especially after abnormal system shutdowns, aligning invocation flags to filesystem-specific recommendations.

- Leverage built-in filesystem journaling and snap-shot capabilities to automate integrity maintenance and recovery.

- Utilize advanced recovery tools like debugfs for ext4 and btrfs restore for btrfs to recover lost content.

- Maintain hardware health monitoring and stable power infrastructure to reduce corruption incidence.

- Integrate routine backup and snapshot schedules into operational workflows to facilitate rollback and restoration.

- Engage with filesystem-specific tuning parameters to optimize consistency guarantees versus performance.

By systematically combining verification, recovery, and prevention, storage systems achieve robustness against corruption events and enhance the availability and reliability vital to modern computing environments.

9.6. System Recovery and Forensics

System recovery and forensic analysis form the corner-stone of modern cybersecurity operations, bridging the gap between incident response and sustained operational integrity. When a compromise occurs, rapid and method-ical recovery processes must be enacted to minimize dam-age, restore services, and extract forensic evidence criti-cal for understanding the root cause and preventing re-currence. This section outlines advanced approaches to system recovery, failover execution, incident log forensics, and postmortem procedures essential for returning systems to trusted states.

Robust recovery begins with a clearly defined failover playbook that prescribes automated and manual procedures tailored to the system architecture and threat profile. Playbooks incorporate tiered response actions triggered by severity levels and incident types. For example, a compromise detected in a database server will invoke containment protocols distinct from those used in a web application breach. Failover mechanisms often leverage redundant infrastructure, such as geographically dispersed data centers or cloud environments configured for active-active or active-passive modes. Transitioning to backup systems requires seamless DNS switching, state synchronization, and verification checks to ensure business continuity without data integrity loss.

Failover playbooks also emphasize isolation of affected components to prevent lateral movement within the network during recovery. This often includes network segmentation updates, reconfiguration of firewall rules, and temporary suspension of vulnerable services. Detailed rollback procedures must be synchronized with system change management to avoid configuration drift and future vulnerabilities. Moreover, maintaining cryptographic integrity of backups and system images is fundamental to ensure that recovery points remain uncompromised.

Incident log forensics play an indispensable role in both guiding recovery and facilitating comprehensive post-incident analysis. Logs collected from intrusion detection systems, firewalls, operating systems, and application layers are aggregated in centralized Security Information and Event Management (SIEM) platforms for real-time correlation and historical review. Effective forensic processes rely on an immutable, timestamped audit trail to reconstruct attack vectors, identify indicators of compromise (IOCs), and profile attacker behaviors. Key challenges include log normalization across heterogeneous sources, filtering noise, and detecting tampering attempts by adversaries who may alter or delete logs to cover tracks.

Advanced log forensic methodologies incorporate timeline analysis, where events are chronologically ordered to expose causality and progression of the attack. This is complemented by memory forensics and disk analysis to recover volatile data and forensic artifacts such as malware signatures or unauthorized modifications. Automated scripts and tools, such as Sleuth Kit or Volatility Framework, augment manual analysis by extracting relevant data structures and highlighting anomalies. Integration of threat intelligence feeds and behavioral analytics further contextualizes findings within global attack trends.

Postmortem analysis is a structured exercise aimed at drilling down into the root causes, assessing the effectiveness of response mechanisms, and deriving actionable lessons learned. This analysis is crucial for continuous improvement of security posture and incident response readiness. Key components include identification of vulnerabilities exploited, evaluation of detection latencies, communication workflows during the incident, and impact on business operations. Formal documentation and debriefings produce After Action Reports (AARs), which outline both technical remediations and process improvements, feeding into policy updates and training programs.

Returning systems to trusted operational states involves

comprehensive validation procedures. Once forensic evidence has been collected and systems have been restored via failover or clean images, integrity verification must confirm that no residual malicious code or misconfigurations remain. Techniques such as cryptographic hashing, secure boot validation, and configuration compliance checks provide assurance of system trustworthiness. In some environments, hardware-based root of trust and Trusted Platform Module (TPM) attestation are employed to confirm firmware and BIOS integrity.

Finally, remediated systems are reintegrated into the production environment following phased verification to ensure stability and security. Continuous monitoring is enhanced post-recovery to detect any resurgence of adversarial activity. Incident learning is institutionalized by updating detection signatures, refining alert thresholds, and recalibrating automated responses to mitigate future attack vectors effectively.

```bash
#!/bin/bash

# Step 1: Isolate compromised network segment
iptables -A FORWARD -s 192.168.10.0/24 -j DROP

# Step 2: Initiate failover to secondary database
     instance
srvctl stop database -d primaryDB
srvctl start database -d secondaryDB

# Step 3: Update DNS entries to point to failover system
nsupdate << EOF
server dns-primary.example.com
update delete db-primary.example.com A
update add db-primary.example.com 300 A 192.168.20.10
send
EOF

# Step 4: Notify operations team
echo "Failover to secondaryDB complete" | mail -s "
     Failover Alert" ops@example.com
```

Output:

253

```
/sbin/iptables: Rule added to drop traffic from subnet 192.168.10.0/24
srvctl: Primary database stopped successfully
srvctl: Secondary database started successfully
nsupdate: DNS entry updated for db-primary.example.com
Mail sent to ops@example.com with subject "Failover Alert"
```

Through synthesis of controlled failover, forensic rigor, and vigilant postmortem analysis, system recovery strategies not only restore functionality but also fortify the security architecture against evolving threats.

Chapter 10

Automation, Scaling, and Best Practices

Scaling success with Alpine Linux requires more than technical mastery—it demands a mindset geared toward automation, continuous improvement, and strategic foresight. This chapter is your playbook for building resilient Alpine fleets and workflows: from hands-off provisioning and policy enforcement to disaster recovery and forward-thinking zero trust deployments. Discover how to weave reliability, compliance, and modern DevOps principles into every layer, future-proofing your infrastructure—no matter how it grows.

10.1. Configuration Management: Ansible, Salt, and Others

Configuration management systems (CMS) have become indispensable in automating the deployment, management, and remediation of infrastructure in modern IT environments. Alpine Linux, known for its minimalistic design and security-oriented philosophy, integrates effectively with leading configuration management tools such as Ansible and Salt, enabling scalable and consistent configuration enforcement across diverse architectures.

The core principle underpinning these tools is the concept of *desired state configuration,* wherein the system's state is defined declaratively and continuously maintained. This approach eliminates configuration drift, a common issue in manual management, while enabling repeatable deployments and systematic updates.

Integration of Ansible with Alpine Linux

Ansible operates on an agentless architecture, communicating over SSH to manage nodes. Alpine Linux's minimal base image results in small attack surfaces and quick deployment cycles, but this minimalism requires explicit preparation to leverage Ansible's full capabilities.

Alpine's default package manager, apk, provides easy installation of Python and OpenSSH, prerequisites for Ansible management. The following standard commands illustrate the preparation of an Alpine node for Ansible control:

```
apk update
apk add python3 py3-pip openssh
rc-update add sshd
service sshd start
```

Alpine's default Python environment requires care because the system's base does not always include python as a binary, often only python3. Ansible modules expect python as the interpreter by default, which can be addressed either by installing a python symlink or explicitly setting the Ansible inventory variable:

```
all:
  hosts:
    alpine-node:
      ansible_host: 192.168.1.100
      ansible_user: root
      ansible_python_interpreter: /usr/bin/python3
```

With these configurations, Ansible can execute playbooks against Alpine nodes, automating package installation, service management, and file deployment. For instance, installing and enabling nginx is succinctly expressed:

```
- name: Install and start nginx
  hosts: alpine-node
  tasks:
    - name: Ensure nginx is installed
      apk:
        name: nginx
        state: present

    - name: Ensure nginx service is running
      service:
        name: nginx
        state: started
        enabled: yes
```

The idempotency features of Ansible ensure that these tasks achieve the target state without performing unintended side effects. Alpine's fast package manager and lean base images contribute to minimal overheads during deployment.

SaltStack Management on Alpine

Salt uses a master-minion architecture, where the Salt master issues commands and manages configurations for minion nodes. To integrate Alpine nodes as Salt minions, the `salt-minion` package must be obtained from community or edge repositories, as Alpine's official repositories do not always package Salt in the main stable channel.

An example installation procedure follows:

```
# Enable community and testing repositories if necessary
echo "http://dl-cdn.alpinelinux.org/alpine/edge/
    community" >> /etc/apk/repositories
apk update
apk add salt-minion python3
rc-update add salt-minion
service salt-minion start
```

Configuration of the minion to point to the Salt master involves editing `/etc/salt/minion`:

```
master: salt-master.domain
id: alpine-node-01
```

Salt's declarative state system, with states written in YAML or Jinja-templated YAML, enables comprehensive desired state specifications. For example, a Salt state to install and configure `nginx` may look like:

```
nginx:
  pkg.installed:
    - name: nginx
  service.running:
    - enable: True
    - watch:
      - pkg: nginx
```

Salt's reactive programming model allows states to trigger service restarts when packages change. The minion securely communicates with the master via ZeroMQ messaging, providing scalable orchestration over hundreds or thousands of Alpine nodes.

Common Best Practices and Challenges

Integrating configuration management within Alpine's unique environment requires attention to several key points:

258

- **Python environment consistency:** Alpine's use of musl libc and minimal Python environments can lead to module compatibility concerns. Pinning Python versions and using virtual environments when necessary can reduce instability.

- **Lightweight security hardening:** Both Ansible and Salt can manage firewall rules, user accounts, and package patches. Alpine's configurations often favor OpenRC over systemd, so CMS playbooks or states must adapt accordingly.

- **Repository and package source management:** Alpine's edge and community repositories are rapidly evolving. Pinning package versions or using internal mirrors ensures stable deployments.

- **Automated updates and drift remediation:** Both Ansible and Salt support scheduling recurrent jobs or orchestrating system updates. This capability is critical for Alpine nodes deployed in production, ensuring that security fixes and performance improvements propagate without manual intervention.

Other Tools and Ecosystem Considerations

Beyond Ansible and Salt, tools such as Puppet and Chef can also be leveraged with Alpine, although these require more complex bootstrapping due to their Ruby dependencies and agents. Lightweight deployment in containerized Alpine environments complements the declarative power of CMS tools by reducing the surface for configuration drift to zero in ephemeral deployments.

In addition, emerging tools like Terraform combined with configuration management permit Alpine nodes to be instantiated and configured as part of unified infrastructure-as-code pipelines, supporting hybrid cloud and edge computing scenarios.

Combining Alpine Linux with advanced configuration management frameworks results in an operational paradigm that is efficient, secure, and reproducible. The synergy between Alpine's minimalistic design and the sophisticated automation capabilities of Ansible, Salt, and similar tools significantly enhances infrastructure reliability and accelerates deployment workflows. Integrating these technologies requires understanding Alpine's unique ecosystem nuances, but the outcome is a robust platform for managing modern distributed systems at scale.

10.2. Scalable System Image Management

Standardized system images form the foundational element for consistent deployment, efficient scaling, and reliable operation across server clusters, containerized environments, and distributed IoT fleets. Achieving scalability in image management requires a cohesive strategy encompassing image construction, distribution mechanisms, and update lifecycles driven by automation pipelines.

The core strategy for scalable system image management begins with defining a minimal, secure base image optimized for the target environment. Alpine Linux, with its lightweight footprint and hardened default configurations, is an exemplary foundation. Construction of these images involves declarative specifications, typically using tools such as mkimage or Dockerfiles tailored for Alpine. Every image variant is version-controlled and parameterized for deployment contexts like server nodes, container runtimes, or embedded device platforms. This approach ensures uniformity, reduces unintentional discrepancies, and simplifies compliance checks.

Automation pipelines are pivotal for the reproducible build process. A continuous integration (CI) framework orchestrates the following logical stages:

1. **Source Retrieval**: Fetch base Alpine releases, security patches, and configuration manifests, integrating vendor advisories in real time.

2. **Image Assembly**: Utilize scripted, deterministic build steps to layer required utilities, security certificates, and device-specific binaries. The layering respects dependency graphs to avoid redundant rebuilds.

3. **Validation**: Automated testing verifies image integrity, boot functionality, and base-level services. For IoT images, hardware-in-the-loop testing can be integrated to confirm compatibility.

4. **Signing and Archival**: Cryptographic signing of images guarantees authenticity. Digitally signed images are archived in versioned registries or artifact repositories with redundancy guarantees.

The CI pipeline can be implemented using widely adopted tools such as Jenkins, GitLab CI, or GitHub Actions. A representative build step employing `docker build` with Alpine might appear as:

```
FROM alpine:3.18
RUN apk add --no-cache openssh bash ca-certificates
COPY config/sshd_config /etc/ssh/sshd_config
CMD ["/usr/sbin/sshd", "-D"]
```

The distribution of built images leverages efficient, secure delivery networks. For containerized environments, container registries like Docker Hub, Amazon ECR, or Google Container Registry provide scalable, geographically distributed endpoints. For server fleets and edge devices, content delivery networks (CDNs) equipped with caching layers optimize image pull latency. Image repositories must support version tagging, rollback, and metadata querying to facilitate operational agility.

For embedded systems and IoT devices that are often offline or have intermittent connectivity, implement differential update mechanisms to minimize bandwidth. Tools such as OSTree or btrfs snapshots combined with delta encoding algorithms enable transferring only binary deltas rather than whole images during updates. This capability is critical for large fleets where network and device resource constraints dominate.

Lifecycle management includes scheduled vulnerability scanning and regular patch integration. Automated vulnerability scanners, such as Clair or Trivy, continuously analyze images to detect outdated packages or known CVEs. Once detected, the pipeline triggers rebuilds and redeployment workflows. Image promotion can follow a staged environment lifecycle moving from development, to testing, and ultimately to production groups with canary release strategies to reduce risk.

A robust update orchestration framework integrates with device management backends or container orchestration platforms like Kubernetes. For the latter, rolling update strategies using Kubernetes Deployments and DaemonSets ensure zero-downtime application of new images. For IoT devices, Over-the-Air (OTA) update agents coordinate with backend image registries and verify signatures before applying updates, with retry and rollback semantics to handle failures.

Algorithm 2 Automated Image Update Workflow

1: Scan existing images with vulnerability database
2: **if** Vulnerabilities found **then**
3:    Trigger image rebuild pipeline with patched packages
4:    Validate rebuilt image
5:    Sign updated image
6:    Publish image to registry/CDN
7:    Notify orchestrator or OTA manager
8:    Implement rolling deployment or OTA update
9:    Monitor update success statuses
10: **else**
11:    Continue monitoring
12: **end if**

The operational benefits of this scalable system image management framework are multifold. Standardized Alpine images ensure consistent baseline security and performance benchmarks. Automation reduces manual intervention, accelerating delivery cycles while mitigating human errors. Versioning and signature-based trust models secure the supply chain and deployment integrity. Distribution infrastructure tailored to environment characteristics guarantees timely image availability irrespective of fleet scale or geographical dispersion. Finally, integrated lifecycle mechanisms ensure all devices and nodes run current, secure software reducing overall risk posture.

Adopting a comprehensive, automated, and secure image management pipeline leveraging Alpine Linux empowers organizations to efficiently scale their infrastructural deployments. The convergence of declarative image specifications, continuous image building and testing, reliable global distribution, and orchestrated lifecycle updates is fundamental to meeting the evolving operational demands of modern server farms, container platforms, and IoT ecosystems.

10.3. Disaster Recovery Automation

Disaster recovery (DR) automation represents a critical evolution in ensuring resilient information systems capable of rapid restoration following adverse events. Automation minimizes human errors, accelerates recovery timelines, and enables consistent execution of complex recovery procedures. The core elements of automated disaster recovery include validating backups, provisioning emergency resources, testing failover scenarios, and orchestrating comprehensive playbooks to guarantee business continuity.

Automated Validation of Backups

Reliable backups are the foundation of any disaster recovery strategy. Automation of backup validation involves systematic verification of backup integrity and consistency to ensure data recoverability. This process typically encompasses cryptographic checksums, restoration of sample data sets into isolated environments, and confirmation of backup completeness according to predefined retention policies.

A common approach is to schedule periodic validation jobs that extract subsets of backup content, restore them in sandboxed instances, and execute integrity checks using hash comparisons or application-level verification scripts. For example, a validation playbook may leverage scripts similar to the following:

```
# Restore database backup to test environment
pg_restore -d test_db /backups/db_backup.dump

# Run data integrity checks
psql -d test_db -f integrity_check.sql

# Compute checksum of critical tables
pg_dump -t critical_table test_db | sha256sum >
    test_checksum.txt

# Compare with baseline checksum
diff test_checksum.txt baseline_checksum.txt
```

Successful completion of these automated tasks increases confidence in backup usability, while failures trigger alerts for immediate attention. Integration with monitoring systems facilitates proactive notification workflows.

Automated Provisioning of Emergency Resources

Disaster recovery demands swift resource allocation, including servers, storage, network configurations, and application deployments. Automation leverages infrastructure as code (IaC) frameworks to declaratively specify and instantiate emergency environments. Tools such as Terraform, Ansible, and cloud-native orchestration services enable repeatable provisioning aligned with DR requirements.

For instance, an IaC script for provisioning virtual machines in a cloud environment can define scaling parameters, network topologies, and security groups, ensuring consistent emergency resource setups. An excerpt from a Terraform configuration may resemble:

```
resource "aws_instance" "dr_server" {
  ami           = "ami-0abcdef1234567890"
  instance_type = "t3.medium"
  subnet_id     = var.subnet_id

  tags = {
    Name = "DR-Emergency-VM"
```

```
    }
}
```

These resources can be dynamically allocated based on trigger conditions such as detection of primary site outages. Automation pipelines can integrate with alerting and ticketing systems to orchestrate provisioning with minimal human intervention.

Testing Failover Scenarios via Automation

Periodic testing of failover procedures is essential to validate DR plan effectiveness and identify latent defects. Manual testing is cumbersome and often impractical in production environments; thus, automation is pivotal for performing controlled, repeatable failover simulations.

Automated failover testing involves triggering predefined recovery workflows that mimic disaster conditions, switching workloads to DR sites or replicas, and verifying service continuity and data consistency. Continuous integration and continuous deployment (CI/CD) pipelines can incorporate failover test stages, leveraging scripting languages and orchestration tools.

A sample playbook written in Ansible for automating failover tests might perform the following sequence:

- Initiate failover on database cluster to standby node.
- Redirect application traffic via load balancer updates.
- Execute health checks against DR infrastructure components.
- Run application smoke tests to confirm functionality.
- Rollback failover if tests indicate anomalies.

Such automation enables frequent failover rehearsals without major operational disruptions, fostering a culture of continual readiness.

Fully Scripted Playbooks for Business Continuity

While individual automation tasks are essential, the unification of these elements into fully scripted disaster recovery playbooks ensures end-to-end orchestration and governance. These playbooks encompass all phases of disaster response-detection, resource provisioning, failover, validation, and restoration-allowing for declarative definitions of workflow dependencies, conditional branching, and rollback procedures.

Playbooks are authored in domain-specific languages or configuration management tools supporting modularity and version control. Integration with monitoring systems provides event-driven triggers, while human-in-the-loop checkpoints afford controlled escalation when necessary.

An example architecture for a DR playbook may include:

1. Detection and Notification: Automatically identify triggering events such as infrastructure failures or cyber incidents.

2. Backup Verification: Execute automated validation to confirm recoverable backups.

3. Resource Provisioning: Instantiate emergency compute, storage, and network resources.

4. Application Failover: Switch workloads to DR infrastructure.

5. Validation and Monitoring: Perform health checks, data integrity tests, and service verifications.

6. Business Continuity Confirmation: Notify stakeholders upon successful recovery.

7. Post-Recovery Cleanup and Reconciliation: Restore primary environment and decommission DR resources.

Leveraging automation frameworks such as Kubernetes Operators, HashiCorp Nomad, or dedicated orchestration platforms enhances scalability and maintainability of the recovery playbooks.

Challenges and Best Practices

Despite its advantages, disaster recovery automation poses challenges related to complexity, test coverage, and environmental drift. To mitigate these, best practices include:

- Employing immutable infrastructure concepts to avoid configuration drift.

- Maintaining version-controlled playbooks alongside infrastructure definitions.

- Incorporating comprehensive logging and audit trails for traceability.

- Regularly updating automation scripts to reflect evolving architectures.

- Establishing clear rollback strategies within play-books to handle partial failures.

Overall, the strategic implementation of disaster recovery automation strengthens organizational resilience by ensuring timely, consistent, and validated recovery actions aligned with business continuity objectives.

10.4. Policy, Compliance, and Auditing at Scale

In extensive and heterogeneous infrastructure environments, automating the enforcement of organizational security policies and compliance reporting is imperative to
maintain consistent security postures and meet regulatory obligations. Manual policy management quickly becomes infeasible due to the volume, variability, and veloc-
ity of change characteristic of large-scale systems. Consequently, automation frameworks are employed to codify
policies, continuously enforce compliance, and produce
verifiable audit trails.

At the core of automated policy enforcement lies *policy-
as-code*, a paradigm which represents governance rules in
machine-readable and executable formats. This approach
allows security policies to be integrated directly into infrastructure deployment workflows, configuration management, and runtime environments. Common policy languages such as Rego (used in Open Policy Agent, OPA)
facilitate fine-grained expression of constraints, ranging
from network segmentation rules to data privacy requirements. When policy checks fail, automated remediation
or alerting mechanisms can be triggered, ensuring rapid
response and reducing human error.

For infrastructure at scale, decentralized enforcement engines running locally on nodes or embedded in microservices enable continuous policy evaluation with minimal latency. These agents synchronize with centralized policy
repositories to receive updates and report compliance status. Such architectures support immutable infrastructure
philosophies, where any deviation from policy manifests
as a detectable drift and an opportunity for automated roll-

269

back or quarantine.

Comprehensive compliance reporting demands aggregation and normalization of data across distributed sources. Audit frameworks standardize the collection of evidence-configuration states, access logs, transaction records, and exception reports-into formats aligned with regulatory schemas such as SOC 2, HIPAA, PCI DSS, and GDPR. Metadata tagging facilitates traceability, enabling auditors and compliance officers to reconstruct the state of controls at any point in time.

The implementation of audit frameworks benefits from an *event-driven* approach, where state changes and security-relevant activities generate immutable events logged to append-only stores or secure ledgers. Technologies like blockchain or tamper-evident log architectures enhance the integrity and non-repudiation properties of audit trails. Automated analysis tools, employing rule-based engines and machine learning, sift through these large datasets to detect anomalies, policy violations, and potential insider threats.

Best practices for regulated environments emphasize the principle of *least privilege* and *separation of duties*, which must be enforced via role-based access control (RBAC) or attribute-based access control (ABAC) integrated into the policy automation framework. Policy automation should include validation of user entitlements before granting access or executing sensitive operations, with all decisions and actions logged for auditability.

To operationalize these concepts, an exemplary compliance automation workflow can be described using the following steps:

- Define organizational policies using a declarative

policy language compatible with the deployment ecosystem.

- Integrate policy enforcement points into CI/CD pipelines, configuration management systems, and runtime environments.

- Deploy lightweight enforcement agents across infrastructure nodes to perform local, real-time policy evaluation.

- Stream all policy evaluation results and security events to a centralized audit aggregation system.

- Normalize and enrich audit data with contextual metadata, tagging by asset, user, and environment.

- Employ rule-based and anomaly detection algorithms to identify compliance violations automatically.

- Trigger automated remediation workflows or escalate incidents to security operations when violations occur.

- Generate periodic compliance reports formatted according to applicable regulatory standards.

- Archive audit data in tamper-resistant storage to maintain integrity and support forensic investigation.

Critical to the success of these automated enforcement systems is the continuous synchronization of policy definitions with evolving regulatory requirements and organizational risk postures. Automated tools should support versioning, testing, and staging of policy changes to prevent inadvertent disruptions.

An example of a policy codification snippet using Rego for restricting inbound network access might look as follows:

```
package infra.network

default allow_inbound = false

allow_inbound {
    input.source == "10.0.0.0/24"
    input.destination_port == 443
}
```

This rule denies inbound traffic except from a trusted subnet targeting HTTPS ports. Such policies are evaluated against real-time network connection attempts, and violations are logged immediately.

In environments subject to stringent audits, establishing an immutable chain of custody for all configuration changes and access requires integrated solutions combining policy enforcement with identity and access management (IAM) and security information and event management (SIEM) systems. The ability to correlate user identities with policy evaluations and corresponding system states underpins forensic investigations and regulatory attestation.

Automating policy enforcement and compliance reporting at scale mandates a convergence of policy-as-code methodologies, distributed enforcement architectures, event-driven audit logging, and integration with security orchestration platforms. This multidisciplinary approach ensures that organizations can uphold stringent security controls ubiquitously, demonstrate adherence to regulatory frameworks efficiently, and rapidly respond to emerging risks without imposing unsustainable manual overheads.

10.5. Continuous Integration/Continuous Deployment (CI/CD)

In Alpine Linux environments, devising Continuous Integration and Continuous Deployment (CI/CD) pipelines requires a distinct approach that leverages the lightweight, security-oriented design of Alpine while preserving robustness, reproducibility, and security across build and delivery stages. Alpine's minimalistic base and musl libc foundation contribute to significantly reduced image sizes and attack surfaces, enabling faster and safer deployments. This section elaborates on orchestrating CI/CD workflows tailored for Alpine, emphasizing build automation, artifact verification, and secure delivery.

Build Automation Optimized for Alpine

The foundation of any CI/CD pipeline is a deterministic and efficient build process. Alpine Linux enforces strict package versioning through its `apk` package manager, facilitating minimal and reproducible build environments. CI pipelines typically employ Alpine base containers, commonly tagged as `alpine:latest` or specific versioned tags, to maintain consistent build images.

To automate builds in Alpine, it is crucial to initialize an environment that installs only essential build dependencies and restricts inclusion of unnecessary tools. This is achieved by crafting Dockerfiles or CI scripts that:

- Start from an Alpine base image.

- Use `apk add --no-cache` to install only required build packages, preventing cache pollution.

- Employ build stages to separate compile-time dependencies from runtime artifacts, minimizing final im-

273

age sizes.

An example Dockerfile snippet for CI build automation in Alpine is:

```
FROM alpine:3.18 AS builder

RUN apk add --no-cache build-base git

WORKDIR /app
COPY . .

RUN make build

FROM alpine:3.18

RUN apk add --no-cache libstdc++

COPY --from=builder /app/bin/myapp /usr/local/bin/myapp

ENTRYPOINT ["myapp"]
```

This multi-stage build pattern ensures that only the final compiled binary and essential runtime libraries reside in the deployment container, improving security and efficiency.

Artifact Verification and Integrity

CI pipelines must incorporate artifact validation mechanisms to guarantee that outputs are trustworthy and reproducible. Common strategies in Alpine-centric CI/CD setups include:

- **Checksum Verification:** Generating cryptographic hashes such as SHA-256 for compiled binaries or packages ensures artifacts have not been altered during transfer or storage. This hash is recomputed and checked at deployment.

- **Digital Signatures:** For production-grade security, signing packages or container images with GPG or other public-key infrastructures enforces provenance checks.

- **Reproducible Builds:** Alpine's stateless package manager and fixed package revisions promote reproducible builds, aiding deterministic artifact production across different build environments.

Implementing checksum verification within CI scripts might appear as follows:

```
# Compute SHA256 checksum of the built artifact
sha256sum /app/bin/myapp > /app/bin/myapp.sha256

# Later in deployment stage: verify checksum
sha256sum -c /app/bin/myapp.sha256
```

Detection of checksum mismatches automatically fails the pipeline, preventing corrupted or tampered artifacts from propagating to deployment.

Secure and Reliable Delivery Workflows

The deployment phase in CI/CD mandates secure and predictable delivery of verified artifacts to target Alpine environments, whether containers, bare-metal systems, or virtualized instances. Strategies to achieve this include:

- **Immutable Infrastructure:** Deploy Alpine containers as immutable units, ensuring deployments replace existing versions atomically rather than updating in-place, reducing configuration drift.

- **Credential and Secret Management:** Utilize dedicated secret stores or CI platform integrations to pass sensitive data securely (e.g., API tokens, repository credentials), avoiding injection into container or pipeline logs.

- **Rolling Updates and Canary Deployments:**

275

Implement deployment strategies that gradually introduce new versions into production, monitoring Alpine container health and performance metrics for anomalies before full rollout.

- **Integration with Alpine Package Repositories:** For organizations maintaining internal Alpine repositories, automating package pushes post-build ensures that deployed artifacts remain consistent with Alpine package management practices.

A secure delivery script segment demonstrating container push and deployment might be:

```
# Authenticate to container registry securely using
    environment-stored token
docker login -u "$REGISTRY_USER" -p "$REGISTRY_TOKEN"
    $REGISTRY_URL

# Tag and push the Alpine-based container image
docker tag myapp:latest $REGISTRY_URL/myapp:ci-
    $CI_PIPELINE_ID
docker push $REGISTRY_URL/myapp:ci-$CI_PIPELINE_ID

# Trigger orchestration system (e.g., Kubernetes)
    deployment update
kubectl set image deployment/myapp myapp=$REGISTRY_URL/
    myapp:ci-$CI_PIPELINE_ID
```

Pipeline Reproducibility and Environment Consistency

To maintain consistency between developer machines, CI runners, and production systems, Alpine pipelines often mandate environment version pinning. Employing explicit Alpine image versions and locking package versions in apk manifests (.abuild files or custom apk repositories) prevents mid-cycle regressions induced by upstream package changes.

CI configuration files can embed this version control with environment specification:

```
stages:
  - build
  - test
  - deploy

variables:
  ALPINE_VERSION: "3.18.4"

build:
  image: alpine:${ALPINE_VERSION}
  script:
    - apk add --no-cache build-base=${ALPINE_VERSION}*
    - make all
```

This approach ensures every CI run executes on a hardened, stable Alpine environment, enhancing reproducibility and traceability.

The orchestration of CI/CD pipelines within Alpine Linux frameworks demands a focused design to uphold lightweight simplicity without compromising robustness. Automation must emphasize minimal build environments, multi-stage container builds, rigorous artifact validation, and immutable, secure deployment workflows. When integrated seamlessly, these principles empower engineering teams to achieve accelerated and reliable software delivery cycles, fully leveraging Alpine's strengths of compactness and security in modern cloud-native architectures.

10.6. Zero Trust and Beyond: Future Proofing Alpine Deployments

The Alpine Linux distribution, renowned for its minimalistic design and security-oriented approach, provides an excellent foundation for implementing modern security paradigms such as Zero Trust Architecture (ZTA). As deployments increasingly operate in environments with dispersed and dynamic infrastructure, embedding Zero Trust principles ensures that trust boundaries are minimized and continuous verification becomes the norm. Future-proofing Alpine deployments requires integrating concepts of immutable infrastructure and harnessing next-generation security mechanisms to preempt adversarial adaptation.

At the heart of Zero Trust is the axiom: never trust, always verify. This contrasts with traditional perimeter-based defense models that implicitly trust internal network entities. In Alpine-based environments, this design philosophy demands that every component, from containerized microservices to host-level processes, authenticate and authorize each interaction based on least privilege. Incorporating mutual Transport Layer Security (mTLS) with stringent certificate management and fine-grained access controls enables Alpine deployments to safeguard communication channels within and across service layers.

Key to operationalizing Zero Trust in Alpine is the adoption of identity-centric security models. Leveraging lightweight Identity and Access Management (IAM) solutions compatible with Alpine's compact footprint, such as SPIFFE/SPIRE or OpenID Connect providers, facilitates automated credential issuance and rotation. This dynamic identity provisioning underpins continuous authentication and policy enforcement, effectively neutralizing the risks posed by stolen credentials or lateral movement. Service mesh technologies like Istio or Linkerd deployed atop Alpine containers further enhance this capability, providing policy-driven traffic encryption and observability essential to Zero Trust network segmentation.

Immutable infrastructure paradigms complement Zero

Trust by ensuring deployed artifacts remain unchanged post-deployment. Alpine's emphasis on a minimal base system and static linking supports the creation of lightweight, reproducible container images or firmware that can be cryptographically verified before execution. Employing Infrastructure as Code (IaC) tools and image signing mechanisms such as Notary or Sigstore enables trustworthiness by design. Rolling updates replace entire nodes or containers rather than patching in place, inherently limiting attack surfaces arising from configuration drift or unauthorized modifications.

Automation plays an indispensable role in maintaining immutable infrastructure within Alpine deployments. Infrastructure provisioning pipelines can integrate automated verification checks for cryptographic signatures and compliance validations, rejecting nonconforming builds. Continuous integration/continuous deployment (CI/CD) workflows orchestrated via Kubernetes operators or Terraform modules ensure Alpine nodes are consistently deployed with the latest validated images and configurations. These immutable patterns not only enforce security posture but also improve operational predictability and rapid disaster recovery capabilities.

Forward-looking Alpine deployments must also engage next-generation security paradigms beyond the current state of the art to withstand evolving threat landscapes. Hardware root of trust features, such as Trusted Platform Module (TPM) integration available on Alpine-supported architectures, enable hardware-based attestation and measured boot processes. This creates a cryptographically verifiable chain of trust from firmware through OS kernel and user space, establishing robust foundations for secure bootstrapping and runtime integrity monitoring.

Extended detection and response (XDR) systems tailored to Alpine's lightweight constraints facilitate advanced behavioral analytics and anomaly detection. By integrating lightweight agents that feed telemetry into centralized analytics platforms, defenders gain real-time visibility and can automate incident response workflows through machine learning-guided playbooks. Ensuring minimal agent footprints and kernel module compatibility are prerequisites for effective adoption without compromising the system's lean nature.

Quantum-resistant cryptography emerges as another critical vector for future-proofing Alpine deployments. Exploring algorithms aligned with NIST's post-quantum cryptography standards prepares data confidentiality and digital signatures for the anticipated advent of quantum computing adversaries. Alpine's modular design permits the selective inclusion of post-quantum cryptographic libraries, thereby enabling incremental transition without wholesale system overhaul.

Actionable steps for securing Alpine deployments with Zero Trust and beyond involve a multi-layered approach:

- **Implement identity-centric authentication and authorization:** Utilize dynamic credential management coupled with mTLS-enabled communication channels to enforce least privilege at all layers.

- **Adopt immutable infrastructure workflows:** Employ IaC, automated signing, and verified image promotion pipelines to eliminate drift and unauthorized code execution.

- **Leverage hardware-based root of trust:** Incorporate TPM and secure boot features to ensure platform integrity from startup through runtime.

- **Deploy service meshes and micro-segmentation:** Use policy-driven service meshes to enforce network segmentation and continuous monitoring within Alpine container environments.

- **Integrate lightweight telemetry agents for XDR:** Enable advanced threat detection through real-time analytics while preserving Alpine's minimal system overhead.

- **Prepare for post-quantum cryptography transition:** Evaluate and integrate quantum-resistant algorithms to future-proof cryptographic operations.

The continuous evolution of threats mandates proactive security architectures that anticipate attacker innovations rather than merely reacting to them. Alpine deployments inherently benefit from a security-first ethos and minimal attack surface, positioning them well for integration with emerging paradigms like Zero Trust and immutable infrastructure. By embracing these principles through automated, verifiable, and hardware-rooted foundations, operators can architect resilient Alpine environments that maintain integrity, confidentiality, and availability amid shifting technological and adversarial landscapes.